EXPOSED

The mark of the

Beast

THE CAPTIVES OF THE DEVIL

Written By

LYDIA E'ELYON

ISBN:
Book cover designed by: JCGC designer
Email: JCGCpublic@outlook.com

Acknowledgment

I would like to thank God for the fervent and humble support of these mighty ones:

Mum Phyllis Magkata, Mrs Nelsiwe Fortunate Dlamini, Bongani Jele, and Thabo Nsibandze.

Without your undeterred support, this work would not soar above the skies to reach the destined reader.

May the grace of our Lord Jesus and His peace overflow to you!

CONTENTS

EXPOSED
The mark of the
Beast

THE CAPTIVES OF THE DEVIL

Preface

This insightful revelatory book exposes the spiritual reality of the underworld. It uncovers the most censored topic about the animal nature of a human being. The animal nature is the very mark of the beast.

This book will give you an insight about how Satan's ancient hatred (Ezekiel 35:5) against humankind began. The ancient hatred is the manifestation of the presence of the devil, which is the beast. The whole revelation about the mark of the beast is unpacked clearly for the very first time.

Get enlightened by this uncompromising truth:

- Understand the manipulating spirit that masquerades itself as a soul, and yet it is the unclean spirit of the ancient wolf –the devil.
- *"Beware of Dogs"* (Philippians 3:2) – ancient evil powers, principalities, rulers and agents of darkness, which stand against the way of the Spirit of Truth to hinder redemption.
- Check yourself through this book, and see if you are not one of *The Captives of the Devil* imprisoned in the underworld, although you may be walking free in

the physical world. Understand that, spiritual life rules the physical life.

Chapter 1

"Never bark at a barking dog"

I t was on a cold Thursday evening, in the month of April 2016. I had an opportunity to preach to a Christian gathering in Boksburg, South. The Holy Spirit was at work, believers expressed their joy, and we all looked forward to our next meeting. It was a very wonderful evening service!

However, after we had driven a distance of about 20 minutes away on the busy highway road from Boksburg to Pretoria, I realized that, there was suddenly a very strange presence of a ravenous predator in the car.

I turned my head and looked at the back seat, but saw nothing. Then I glanced at the face of the lady pastor that I had travelled with, thinking that maybe she is also sensing the strange presence. Nevertheless, she kept a straight face under her eyeglasses, and focused on the car mirror. She drove on, and said nothing.

The brutal beast is in the car

Whilst perplexed by the strange presence, my spiritual eye opened to see what carried the strange presence. I saw an open vision of a very huge angry black furry beast that looked very brutal. It looked like a wild dog *(untameable)*, sat at the backseat of the car behind my back.

The way it fumed, seemed like it wanted to ravage me. Upon seeing its angry reaction, I placed my hand on my head, and pleaded the Blood of Jesus Christ to cover me. Puzzled about the whole thing, and wondering about how the angry giant wolf jump into the car?

Then I heard the Lord speaking to me:

"Do you remember the leader who raged against you at the church where you are coming from?"

My mind quickly flashedback, and I recalled her reaction. Then, the Lord said to me, *"This is her spirit, the ravenous wolf you see."*

At that moment, the strange presence left the car.

Evident in the reaction

I never thought that, a spirit of a human being could become a wolf. This is not an easy thing to suspect, and neither to comprehend. When you relate with a person, you relate with his/her spirit, but not the physical form you see. But, what is the actual form of the spirit of a human being, because even a ghost is hardly seen with physical eyes?

Oh! How sweet, friendly, and always befriended, and yet unclean is the spirit of a dog. The leader in question was very nice to me as she also welcomed us very well.

She also came up to join those who wanted a prayer. We even spoke a little about their leadership problems in the church, and how I was to help; but nothing was suspicious about her character at all.

However, during prayer when I laid my hands on her, I picked that, there was something wrong with her. She became a little furious, and kept disturbing my attention by flapping her arms and telling me:

"Woman of God scan! Scan me; see if there is any evil in my heart."

It was annoying like in the case of the fortune-teller slave girl, who kept following Paul and Silas and crying out,

"These are the servants of Jehovah El Elyon" –the Most High God (Acts 16:17).

She was speaking through an evil spirit, but not by the Holy Spirit. Well, I did not give much attention to that, until I was very far away from the church, where her evil came pursuing me with evil intents.

Ravaged Unaware

Now, it happened on the following week, that the possessed woman composed false accusations to tarnish my character within a short space of time. What have I done really? I wondered.

The false accusations were believable, but grievous to me. In my heart, I knew that I was innocent of such false accusations. Nevertheless, how do you convince other people that you are innocent?

People easily believe a lie more than the truth. If I had demanded and collected money offerings like most preachers do, then accused of collecting much, I would not care. However, I did not even ask for money to buy the car fuel.

It is better when people make noise about something that you have done, so that you may correct your error, than nailed for doing good.

I thank God for this incident, because that is where my mind paused a while, to study carefully the lives of those who rise in oppositions, as the one that I had encountered; and the spirit that they have. A wise man of God who heard my side of the story, advised me with thought provoking words, and he said,

"Never bark at a barking dog!"

I raised my eyebrows, *"Did the man of God say that?"*

Sometimes a wolf moves amongst the sheep and the goats. It is a spiritual identity of evil characters, and practises of some people. However, the church is silent about this, although Jesus spoke about it, and the scriptures talk about dogs/ wolves several times in the bible.

As you continue to read about this revelation, you will discover why the church is quiet about *–the spirit of the wolf.*

Chapter 2

The Predator of the Sheep

Spot the evil spirit of a persecutor

I raved about with these questions in my mind: Why this kind of outrage? What is it that backs such a rage against the Christians?

What causes a human being to rise with envy against another human being to the point of shedding blood? When evening comes and night falls, people fear fellow human beings more than the darkness itself.

In the course of the day or night, people spend their time scheming evil against others, than discerning the deeds of their hands. See clearly how the contender of your soul takes it to captivity.

A frenzied sound near your house fills your heart with dread, *"A thief."*

A knock of a stranded traveller at night causes one to spring up with an axe on your hand before blaring, *"Whose there?"* What causes suspicions amongst fellow human beings? Why do they rise in rage against fellows like animals?

Whilst I pondered about the unhuman nature of a human being, the Holy Spirit led me to read a verse in the Bible, and I read it with great concern:

*"**Why do the heathen rage** and the people imagine a vain thing? The kings of the earth set themselves, and the **rulers take counsel together, against the LORD, and against his anointed,** saying, Let us break their bands asunder, and cast away their cords from us"* (Psalms 2:1-3).

Then, the Holy Spirit led me to read the book of Acts chapter 4. Whilst reading, my eye opened, and I grasped that, the early Apostles read the same

15

Psalms 2:1-3 when they faced persecutions – *troubled by the spirit of a dog.*

The bible says, they lifted up their voice to God with one accord, and said,

"Lord, you are God, which has made heaven, and earth, and the sea, and all that in them: Who by the mouth of thy servant David hast said: **Why did the heathen rage** *and the people imagine vain things? The kings of the earth stood up, and the rulers were gathered together against the Lord and against His Christ" (Acts 4:24-26).*

My eye became more enlightened. I began to realize that, persecutions are common against the sheep, and the shepherds of the sheep of the LORD Jesus.

Therefore, it did not start with me, although I can foresee the end of it. Although you may suffer thus, these are not direct attacks against you as a believer, but they are against the Name –Jesus Christ –the Redeemer.

Why do they rage?

Jesus foretold the rise of the spirit of Dog. He prophesied that, believers shall be persecuted for His name.

*"But before all these things, **they will lay their hands on you and persecute you, delivering you up to the synagogues and prisons.** You will be brought before kings and rulers **for My name's sake"*** (Luke 21:14).

You may have at some point, or on several occasions faced unwavering oppositions and persecutions by fellow human beings. The book of Acts 25:7 reveal false accusation levied against Apostle Paul.

However, this was not the first or last time he was falsely accused. The records state that these false accusations were many. However, authentic evidence by the Holy Spirit proved them false:

And when he arrived, the Jews which came down from Jerusalem stood round about, and laid many and GRIEVOUS complaints against Paul, **which they could not prove** (Acts 25:7).

The dogs rage against the anointed one, and they fight against the Gospel of Jesus Christ, because it has the full package for restoring man to his former right condition as the image of God. The original image of God does not have the strange creature –unhuman nature/ spirit of a dog.

The Revelation about the Ancient Beast

My heart was compelled to ask the LORD to give me more revelation and understanding about the character of predators –that strange creature in a human being. Why is there such raucous veal against the sheep?

At that very hour whilst petitioning the LORD, I heard a tremendous sound of a roaring thunder rumbling on the floor of the house. I thought that maybe there was a sudden heavy rain.

Due to the intensity of the thunder, I checked through the window, but to my surprise, busked rays of the orange-yellow sun on the cloudless beautiful blue sky is all that I saw. But, why did it thunder?

"The LORD thundered from heaven; the voice of the Most High resounded amid the hail and burning coals" (Psalms 18:13).

There I began to feel a strong presence of the LORD. He told me that, He has heard my prayer, and He will reveal to me everything about the beast. That spirit of the devil that causes rebellion, persecutions, and lawlessness.

Precept by precept, the Spirit of the LORD began to reveal the dog to me, *–synonym with a* *wolf.* It took me about two years to have full understanding, until I discovered that, this is the ancient wolf –the devil.

I termed it, '*the dread of the Shepherd and predator of the sheep.'* This drove me to the great revelation about the ancient beast, and its mark. I found means to overcome dogs as taught by Christ Jesus.

It attacks through dreams

During that time of receiving the revelations, I began to experience attacks by many different wolves and dogs in my dreams.

These incidents became frequent in my dreams and visions to the point that, I started getting worried about; why do wolves fight against me in the dream?

Nevertheless, in all the dreams, I wrestled and killed the leader of the pack of wolves, and the rest of the wolves ran away from me.

On the 22 February 2017, I had a very great fight with a black bulldog that looked like a mighty bear. I saw myself walking up a hill, and as I was moving up along the way this bulldog came prowling to attack me.

In the dream, the Spirit of the LORD came mightily upon me to give me courage and strength. At that moment, another black bulldog appeared in front of the first one, which looked like a bear, and it raised itself in a vicious attack against me, but I grabbed it with my two hands.

It opened its mouth to bite me, and behold I saw inside its mouth –*it had teeth as of a human being*. Quickly, with the mighty strength of the Lord, I lifted it up, and threw it away.

It fell headlong on the ground with its face buried on the ground, and its hind legs flying wide spread in the air. Yah! Great was its death, bravo Holy Spirit!

Now, at that very moment of my victory, the dogs increased in number and they became six ferocious dogs in a bid to kill me.

The other black bulldog that appeared at first tried to resurrect the dead bulldog, so that they may all attack me. However, even more, the Spirit of the LORD came upon me and I began to decree, "*You must all die by the Name of Jesus.*"

Suddenly, all the dogs died and none of them lived again. Then I continued to walk up the hill. After the Spirit of the Lord said to me,

"Unless your spiritual eye is opened, you will not be able to see how much power you have been given from above, to conquer."

The dog that spoke perplexed me

His words reverberated in my ears repeatedly. I saw another dreadful vision. In this vision, there were many wolves (dogs) gathered against me along a barrier line, where they were not even supposed to pass. Nevertheless, is this not written in the book of Isaiah?

*"And indeed they shall surely gather together, but not because of Me. **Whoever gathers against you shall fall for your sake"** (Isaiah 54:15).*

Again, the Lord gave me strength to fight them. I grabbed the leader of the group of dogs, and dashed him against the wall. I marvelled because the wolf spoke, and cried out:

"Haai! Elohim (elohim), you are now killing us without mercy."

After it spoke those words to me, that wolf died instantly. Praise the LORD! The rest of the dogs fled from the scene. I became perplexed. Why did this dog speak words like a person who is religious or spiritual? It pronounced Elohim clearly.

Do animals speak words like human beings? How so is it, that a dog clearly pronounces the awesome word –Elohim? This vision disturbed me very much, and I became paranoid.

The Meaning of Dogs in a Dream

I woke up again, and asked the Lord about the frequency of these kinds of scenes in my dreams.

I enquired of the LORD about the meaning of Elohim with relation to humankind, because the dog was actually talking to me.

He gave me dream interpretations for every wolf event that I saw. He said that the wolf/s represent a person /people who are not born of the Spirit of God *–they are in their old nature that is hostile to God and unhuman.*

I pleaded to know more about the relationship between man, and the wolf. Why a wolf? How did the spirit of a dog take full possession of the human soul, such that it transformed its being to a human? The Lord began to enlighten me through scripture as I am about to write to you in the following chapters of this Book. Indeed, unless I had learned how to conquer the beast, so that I may draw humankind to Christ, how vain is my mission to preach the Gospel?

As you continue to read the book, you will learn about kinds of dogs, so that whenever you dream about a dog, you will be able to relate it with the kind of a person of that spirit. Are you perplexed, because wicked people pursue you? You give up and run away, because all you can see is wicked people?

You must understand the spirit behind them, and then you will boldly stand in the Name of Jesus, and face that dog like David against Goliath. The dog presides with a human soul as the spirit of the human, but it can be chased away, to let the original spirit of the "image of God" to emerge.

Then all people can live in harmony without suspecting one another. Believers who get the revelation in this book, subdues the world of sin, that dominated by the unhuman spirit. This revelation as it continues to unfold, gives details about the mark of the beast written about in scriptures.

It is an identity of a dog

A wolf and a dog are of the same family. Understand based on this revelation, that the statement of the Lord Jesus about wolves and dogs in the bible is not a proverb.

There is no better way to mention that someone is a dog, and there is no lesser way to say that someone is a sheep.

A dog is a dog and will never be a sheep. The people of the world understand what a dog is, and they easily identify its characters than the children of the light who are ever running away from dogs.

The people of the world refer to each other as dogs, because they know themselves. The Samaritan woman understood what Jesus was talking about as He spoke in this manner about dogs (Matthew 15:26-27): He answered,

*"It is not right to take the children's bread and throw it to the **little dogs.**"*

She said, *"Yes, Lord, yet even* **the little dogs** (whelps) eat the crumbs that fall from their young masters' table."

There was a time when God considered the Jews as lost sheep, because they had polluted themselves with the unclean practises of the Gentiles (Dogs) through which as a result their land vomited them out.

At the revealing of the Messiah –Jesus Christ, the children of Israel had completely backslidden, and they received the spirit and mark of the beast like most of the Pharisees, Sadducees, Scribes, Lawyers, and many priests.

They became the captives of the devil with the lawless spirit of a dog. Everyone was doing as he pleased. At the appointed time, the Lord Jesus faced the Pharisees and rebuked them because of the wolf nature that they harnessed within themselves.

Although they boasted about Abraham and Prophet Moses, but they preached what they did not practise, because the dog spirit was at work in them.

You cannot please God under such control by this unclean creature. The dog within you will begin to bark. The Spirit of God as He was with Moses who wrote the Torah was not testifying in Pharisees –even though they taught those things.

Today, preachers preach about the power of God, and saying that they are not ashamed of the

Gospel. Nevertheless, when a test comes to demonstrate that power of God, they begin to fall under the hand of the spirits of dogs.

They compromise and support the acts of apostasy *as those who controlled by the spirit of dogs do.* There is no need to live a compromised life in order to build relationships with rebels. If you are a believer, be a true believer.

"Outside are the dogs *and sorcerers and the sexually immoral and murderers and idolaters, and everyone who loves and practices falsehood"*(Revelation 22:15).

Jesus showed the Pharisees that, He was aware of their false identity. He knew what they are capable of doing. People who have the dog identity do these things: They persecute believers and kill prophets.

"Indeed I send you prophets, wise men, and scribes; some of them you will kill and crucify, and some of them

you will scourge in your synagogues and persecute from city to city (Matthew 23:34-36).

Scars of the dog bite

I had often made mistakes of trusting too much, and embracing everybody that comes my way without first testing their spirit. As a result, dogs had bitten me many times.

It was then after the Boksburg incident and this revelation, that I began to master how to identify and overcome dogs.

Before then, I suffered disappointments because; I didn't know that I was dealing with a dog in some people's characters.

Most of them can easily notice your innocence and purity of heart. That is why they come pouncing and prowling to destroy your soul.

Never trade your righteous innocence for dust, because dogs will drag, and trod you on the mud, your healing may become difficult afterwards.

It does not matter how much some people seem to celebrate you because of the miracles that the Lord Jesus performed through you.

Keep humble and walk on the footsteps of the Lord Jesus without putting your trust on anybody.

Take time to know a person, before trust

Jesus in His days on earth did not trust anyone. Even when people celebrate you, find out, who are these people who are rejoicing with you? It might happen that in the midst of them are ravenous dogs. Do what Jesus did:

*"When He was in Jerusalem during the Passover Feast, many believed in His name after seeing His signs (wonders, miracles) which He was doing. **But Jesus did not entrust Himself to them**, because He*

knew all men; And He did not need anyone to bear witness concerning man <u>for He Himself knew what was in man</u>" (John 2:23-25).

Jesus came to earth knowing already the strange nature in humankind *(the predatory spirit)*.

That is why He came to save all who believed in Him. Yes, He carried the full package of redemption to set free all who are in such an evil nature.

Those who are not born again of the Spirit of God have this spirit of a dog fully controlling their souls.

No matter how pure is your heart towards some people, because they show you kindness, never makes yourself an easy access to them.

You do not know what spirit makes them to be kind. At least the Lord Jesus could scan their hearts (spirits) as stated in the verse:

"He did not need anyone to bear witness concerning man for He Himself knew what was in man" (John 2:25).

Jesus was not deceived or moved by their celebration or joy over His miracles or their good idea to make Him king.

The problem with this evil spirit of a dog is that, it always deceives people. Frown at anyone that wants to promote you to something else because of your great works.

That is a controlling spirit of a dog, and it has only one motive –*to use you for its purposes and derail you from your heavenly mission.* Reject deceptive human elevations.

"For promotion comes neither from the east nor from the west nor from the south, but God is the judge: He demotes one, and elevates another" (Psalms 75:6-7).

As a child of God and a soul winner for Jesus Christ, you must also remember to present Him well with your countenance before those who are captives of the devil.

Remember that in as much as they are carrying a very hostile evil spirit against believers, they are not under its control by their will.

Many have found themselves already in this nature from birth, like you before you were born again. Therefore, show compassion, so that, their souls may be set free from this cage.

At the same time, do not behave funny, or treat with contempt those you meet for the first time because of their suspicious behaviours or how they look.

Contempt blocks your light from shining to expel the darkness in people if there is any –*that unclean spirit of a dog.*

Let the Holy Spirit search the hearts of your acquaintances as you shine forth your light, even with your godly countenance.

Your light overcomes darkness when you are with people, but not the many words you speak or funny attitude. Words without light are like blunt swords.

A mountain full of blunt swords does not give hope for rescue. Therefore, a profane word from an evil heart is like a deadly disease.

The light shines more brilliant when you maintain a quiet spirit in the midst of your acquaintances. You might better listen more, and discern more than exhorting someone that you are not so very sure of his or her spirit.

At the right time, speak to edify the right spirit once proven to be a right spirit; rebuke every unclean spirit without giving them any hope and expectation of comfort or sign of kindness.

You will be hated

Never entertain or show partiality to unclean spirits. Do not fear if tagged *'a difficult person.'* If you are to overcome the power of the dog, then, never mind counterblasts. Otherwise, you will develop grievous scars in your spirit, which may be hard to heal.

It is very important for you to have a clear understanding about the origin of the spirit of the wolf, as it dominates many people.

This devil did not originate with the human soul from the beginning, but it is a spirit of hatred from Satan. At the time of the Lord Jesus in the world, Satan's ancient hatred manifested itself with great intensity.

The unrelenting hatred of Satan against humankind advanced even more after Jesus rose from the dead. As a believer, expect hatred from those possessed by the spirit of the wolf, because they are of the devil.

"And you will be hated by all for My name's sake" (Matthew 10:22).

Study the following account about the creation of man, and find out how through hatred, Satan planted the evil spirit of the wolf in the human's soul.

The wolf takes the form of a human being – *mind, body and spirit,* and thus creating a blasphemous creature that is unhuman –opposing the original image of God.

Chapter 3

The Ancient Hatred

Why Satan hates human beings

On the right side of the table where God was creating humankind, stood the angels created out of fire and light. Archangel Michael led them. On the left hand side, stood the angels created of the deep darkness, and Lucifer led them.

God presented man as self-identification of the Father, Son, and Holy Spirit whilst still in a form of mud.

Introducing the lifeless moulded mud to the angels, God said, *"Behold the Man! Worship My image!"*

Meaning, give honour and service to God's image –for he is a god. The LORD reminds man about his identity through the Psalm of David:

"I said, you are gods (elohim) and all of you are children of the Most High"* (Psalm 82:6). The Lord Jesus also defended the *'god'* status of humankind and He said, "*Is it not written in your law,"* **"I said, you are gods?"** *"If He called them gods, unto whom the word of God came, and the scripture cannot be broken*" (John 10:34-35).

The bible says, *When God brought the first born into the world, He said,* **"Let all the angels of God worship him"** (Hebrew 1:6).

Then, all the rest of the creation stood up in awe of man, they rhymed with great joy, blessing the LORD God for His image.

The greatest leaders of the throngs of angels of the LORD made of light, rendered relevant service to the man from that time, and they gave glory to God for His wonderfully made image.

The service of angels is worship and humility to humankind for they cannot do much without the spiritual composite. This becomes a collaboration of heaven and earth, the spiritual and the physical giving great glory to God.

Unlike man who is made of both the spirit and the dust of the earth, man needs angelic or spiritual assistance to maintain his spiritual life, so that he may strengthen his mortal body.

It is a great abomination for an angel to demand worship from man, because, there is nothing of the earth that they are made of, for them to desire.

God commanded angels to service the spiritual needs of humankind as enablement. Angels abide in heaven, and they know the necessary resources and storehouses, which keeps the important things needed by man on earth.

Angels are to worship (serve) man with those spiritual things as commanded by God, whilst man serve God on earthly matters assigned to him by the same God. When angels refuse to serve man, it becomes an unpardonable sin against God.

Lucifer rebelled God's commandment to worship man

The introduction or presentation of man as elohim gave an uncontrollable shiver to Lucifer. The term *'god'* in the Hebrew context is elohim. Elohim means –the mighty one, judge, and ruler of an estimable realm.

Lucifer could not accept that God elevated mud to be like God, and on top of that, worshipped. He envied man and became very distressed. Whilst the rest of the angels served the man on the creation table, Lucifer stood aloof and refused to serve.

From thence, because of his rebellion, envy, and hatred, Lucifer fell from his glory, and he became Satan –*the envious and evil one,* whilst man became elohim –*the mighty one, judge, and ruler of the earth.*

God created elohim –His image to manifest the kingdom of God on earth as it is in heaven, fulfilling His word when He said, "Let US create man in Our own Image and in Our Likeness" (Genesis 1:26). It would be impossible for man to rule the earth without the God like ability.

However, Satan began to hate man on this account. Then he influenced thousands of angels under his domain of leadership to disobey God's command to worship humankind.

He promised them to established a throne above the stars of God (Isaiah 14:13-21). When you take a brief tour through spiritual history, you will be very surprised to know those stars of God.

When humankind was dedicated and officially introduced to the hosts of angels, he was still lifeless mud on the creation table of God. Praising God for something that is not yet, and giving it that much honour became a thoughtless thing to Satan.

However, it is God's habit to praise what is not yet, as though it exists. When the praise goes before Him, He calls forth those things He has created in His Alpha Omega imagination.

There comes in the faith of God, but darkness does not comprehend such things, and so, Satan revolted even more. Adam did not see the revolt of Satan against him.

Praise be to God, as the preacher said, *"The dead know nothing."* He did not hear nor perceived any complain against him.

He was as good as an innocent new born baby in deep sleep, surrounded by the Angels of the LORD all around, administering to his muddy body.

This is the same attitude that God expects of you after you are born again. To die in the flesh, and live in the Spirit, so that you do not allow the spirit of the wolf to establish a throne over your mind. After completing to create humankind –male and female, God blessed them and said,

"Be fruitful, and multiply, and replenish the earth, and subdue it: and have dominion over the fish of the sea, and over the fowl of the air, and over every living thing that moves upon the earth" (Genesis 1:28).

After blessing them, then there was a very big bang as God: Breathed into his nostrils the breath of life, and man became a living being (Genesis 2:7).

Halleluiah! Praise be the Most High God. Yes! God did it, and Satan became confounded. When

Adam woke up from his slumber, he found a revolt, and did not understood the cause, but neither did he even care.

"I lay down and slept; I awoke, for the LORD sustained me, I will not be afraid of ten thousands of people who have set themselves against me all around me" (Psalm 3:5-6).

Then God took the man –Adam and put him in the Garden of Eden which was on the Eastern part of His highest heaven to tend and keep it (Genesis 2:15). God visited Adam daily in the cool of the day, at about 3.00 PM.

Satan marked the hours of God's visit, so that, he may gain entry against the man before time. According to the sundial, the hours of visitation were as follows:

- 1500 Hrs world time
- 9 AM on the western

- 12 PM on the north
- 6 AM on the Southern regions of the underworld

Test must come

Adam was only keeping God's garden that He planted in Eden. This was not Adam's garden nor his promised permanent residence, but a place of trial. Therefore, in the Garden of Eden, Adam was just a man still under God's making.

In the hours of visitation, God had fellowship with him, to give him laws and instructions to abide by. He taught him many things including how to remain as His image.

To be creative, and fruitful as His Likeness, and how to acquire the promise to govern the earth. The LORD teaches a person how to obey His commandments, and gives him warning about the dangers of disobedience.

However, a person must pass through tests to see if he will indeed obey commandments. God may not tell you by whom the test will come. This is because a test is a trial to measure the maturity of the mind and spirit of man with just scales.

Once you pass the test, then He authorizes you over His will according to the measure that He has found. Failing God's test may cause you to fall on the hand of the devil, so that he may fulfil his will over your life.

Whenever there is an evil agenda against a righteous person, the Holy Spirit sends a warning and some precepts to follow.

He knows beforehand what the enemy is planning. Commandments are not intimidating strict restrictions, but guidelines to protect and keep a person from the evil plan of the enemy. Here is an example:

"The ones that fell on the good ground are those who, having heard the word with a noble and good heart, keep it and bear fruit with patience."

Follow the warnings of the LORD and His commandments with perseverance, not forgetting to discern your weak points. Then you will have victory during temptations and trials, and become God's star!

"And the LORD God commanded the man, saying; "Of every tree of the garden you may freely eat; but of the tree of the knowledge of good and evil you shall not eat, for in the day that you eat of it you shall surely die" (Genesis 2:16-17).

God loves, and has good thoughts towards all His people. He does not want to see anyone of them fall into the cage of the devil, not even one. As a result, He gives warnings, commandments, and careful instructions to anyone beforehand, and just on time. Innocent are those who carefully consider what God has said, and do it without argument.

"Every word of God is pure; He is a shield to those who put their trust in Him" (Proverbs 30:5).

Many are crying foul because the devil oppresses them. Nevertheless, if only they heeded, no evil would have overtaken them.

A depraved attitude towards the word of the LORD leads many to sin. The parable of the Lord Jesus in Luke 8:11-15 describes depraved attitudes of hearts of people towards God's word. Jesus explained each depraved attitude that causes failure during tests:

I.   Those *by the wayside* are the ones *who hear; then the devil comes and takes away the word out of their hearts, lest they should believe and be saved.*

II. The ones *on the rock* are those who, when they hear, receive the word with joy; and these *have no root,* who *believes for a while and in time of temptation fall away*.

III. The ones that fell *amongst thorns* are those who, when they have heard, go out and are *shocked with cares, riches, and pleasure of life, and bring forth no fruit to maturity*.

The Bursting Antagonism and Pride of Satan

Satan did not rejoice to see humankind elevated from dust, and served by angels as the affirmation of *Genesis 1:26-28*. He thought of himself superior to man, because God formed him out of the darkness that covered the face of the deep (subterranean).

"And darkness covered the deep waters" (Genesis 1:2).

The 'deep' is the furthest destination underneath the core that holds the mighty waters underground. This place existed before God established the earth above it, and before the creation of humankind.

Satan considered himself worthy to rule over all the things, which God created. God formed Lucifer (Satan) through the deep darkness, so that he may rule over darkness, unlike the angels, which He formed through fire and light (Genesis 1:16).

After his rebellion, the LORD revoked his power to rule darkness, and He made light to rule over Satan and darkness. Many people think that Satan is very bright and beautiful. It is no longer so.

Although staying in heaven once made him to glow in beauty and excellent look, because God dressed him with expensive jackets adorned with precious stones – the sardius, topaz, diamond, beryl, onyx, and the jasper, sapphire, emerald, and the carbuncle, and gold (Ezekiel 28:13-19).

However, because of pride, he fell, and his beauty faded. His eyes shrivelled like a black dog's face. His precious stones coverings became tatters, and the precious stones crushed to fine dust.

Today, his complexion is charcoal ash smoke. However, he masquerades as an angel of light (2 Corinthians 11:14). Satan disguises himself as an angel of light, to manipulate the power of light that subdues darkness.

As formed through the deep darkness, when he rebelled against God, heaven vomited him back to deep darkness.

There he exists as an underworld subject of Death. He is a servant of Death with a task to pull people back to dust.

He attends funerals in his black tunic, and dances there all night by the tomb of the dead. That is the only time when Satan rejoices against humankind *–when they die*. Especially when they die in darkness, and not born again of water and the Holy Spirit.

Satan's Protests against Humankind

By looking at how Adam and Eve were keeping up and excelling daily in the Garden of Eden; Satan smoked with envy and perpetual rage against them. He vented out his grievance to God, protesting against three things:

1. God's order given to angels instructing them to worship (serve) humankind, who is a disposable living being, created from the remains of the earth.
2. God's fellowship and visit to humankind
3. God's blessing and commandment to the contemptible humankind, to rule the earth and all its living things.

This is the record of Satan's protest against God's commandment:

*"When I consider Your heavens, the works of Your fingers, the moon and the stars, which you have ordained, **what is man that you are mindful of him, and the son of man that you visit him?***

***For you have made him a little lower than the angels (made of dust), yet you have crowned him with glory and honour.** You have made him to have dominion over the works of your hands* [Genesis 1:26-31];

***You have put all things under his feet**, all sheep and oxen –Even the beasts of the field, the birds of the air and the fish of the sea that pass through the paths of the sea"*(Psalm 8:3-8).

Satan's First Attack against Humankind

Having thus protested, God gave Satan up to implement violent attacks against humankind.

"Behold he is in your hand, but spare his soul" (Job 2:6).

There came the time of testing God's first image, to prove the lustre of his star. This became the most difficult test, because God Himself schooled Adam.

However, Adam did not directly withstand the devil in the test, because through deceit he took advantage of his weak point *–the woman.*

"So God drove out the man; and He placed cherubim at the east of the garden of Eden, and a flaming sword which turned every way, to guard the way to the tree of life" (Genesis 3:24).

The star did not continue to shine. The devil managed to diminish the glory of its lustre, with an aim to construct his throne over Adam's head, making him lesser of what God said he is. But, how far did this evil plan go?

Chapter 4

The Genesis of the Mark of the Beast

The first attack against humankind did not seem to work well for Satan, although it resulted in their expulsion from Eden.

God's favour and compassion on man confused, and harassed the Devil. Seeing Adam and Eve still living and farming on the earth far away from the lucrative Garden of Eden, did not cheer him up.

Whenever seeing Adam freely ploughing his new garden, strategies of antagonism arose in Satan's heart. He realised that driving out the man from Eden became a big breakthrough to the man. He meant it for evil, but God turned it for their good. As the scripture says that,

"We are assured and know that God being a partner in their labour *all things work together and are fitting into* a plan for good to and for those who love God and are called according to His design and purpose. For those whom He foreknew of whom He was aware and loved beforehand, He also destined from the beginning foreordaining them to be moulded into the image of His Son and share inwardly His likeness, that He might become the firstborn among many brethren.

And those whom He thus foreordained, He also called; and those whom He called, He also justified (acquitted, made righteous, putting them into right standing with Himself). And those whom He justified, He also glorified [raising them to a heavenly dignity and condition or state of being]. What then shall we say to [all] this? If God is for us, who can be against us? [Who can be our foe, if God is on our side?] [Ps. 118:6.] (Romans 8:28-31).

Satan missed the point

The Garden of Eden was not Adam's original destination according to what God purposed for man. However, it was a temporal residence for him to learn the ways of the Lord. Scheming in his wicked thoughts, it quickly ticked on the mind of Satan:

The people will have the legal right to exercise their authority to dominate the whole earth and to subdue it as God promised them. For after all, God never said that, man must fill the Garden of Eden, but fill the earth:

"Let Us make man in Our image, according to Our likeness; let them have dominion over the fish of the sea, over the birds of the air, and over the cattle, over all the earth and over every creeping thing that creeps on the earth. So God created man in His own image; in the image of God He created them. Then God blessed them, and God said to them, "Be

fruitful and multiply; fill the earth and subdue it" (Genesis 1:26-28).

Satan realised that humankind found favour with God. God kept His promise to make man dominate the earth, after He drove them out of Eden.

The enemy was confounded, because the curse, which came by the temptation of the serpent, turned to a blessing to this man and his wife (Adam and Eve). They began to prosper in all their ways and even began to have children.

David the most discerning and God fearing king who perceived the ways of the LORD God; once spoke these words when Shimei the son of Gera came to curse him continually:

"It may be that the LORD will look on my affliction, and that the LORD will repay me with good for his cursing this day" (2 Samuel 16:12).

The scripture says, the man continued to curse and kick the dust against David, but he said no evil word in response to that curse, instead he said:

"If he is cursing because the Lord said to him, "Curse David," who then shall ask, why have you done so?" (2 Samuel 16:10).

The spirit of a dog causes a person to rise in opposition against another over a trifle. With reference to the above verse, you will understand that, God allows the adversary to do so against the upright. Nothing that happens under the sun, unless permitted spiritually as Jesus once said:

"You would have no power over me at all unless it was given to you from above" (John 19:11), (Leviticus 26:19), (Job 1:12).

There is a kind of opposition, which you must not fight back. It has come to move you to your original destiny, or to promote you. Nevertheless, keep your eyes focused to the One who judges all spirits, *the great Elohim*.

Do not fight for yourself, because Jehovah Sabaoth, the Lord of host, musters His army to defend the upright when attacked. He is excellent and mighty in battle. In a similar case as against Job, Satan again grumbled before God about the new establishment and dominion of Adam and Eve on the huge and fruitful planet earth.

"Have You not made a hedge around his household, and around all that he has on every side? You have blessed the works of his hands, and his possessions have increased in the land" (Job 1:10).

Satan's plan to annihilate the human race

God did not pay any positive attention to the grievances of Satan against man, because they sprang from envy. Envy is evil and it leads to covetousness, defrauding, stealing, murder, and annihilation of innocent souls.

Therefore, these grievances became a great iniquity before God. Considering all the compassion of God towards His image, the enemy dreaded the shadow of what was to befall him. He considered that God has proclaimed a curse against the serpent that deceived Eve.

"The Seed of the woman will crush the head of the serpent."

Although he was not very sure about the seed of the woman there, but he clearly understood that, the head of the serpent was himself. Spiritually, a *'Head'* symbolises a leader, and the *tail* refers to a follower/s.

In this case, the head of rebellion and the deception that tempted Eve is Satan. The tail is the group of fallen angels of darkness who followed him. These became devils or evil spirits.

"I will put enmity between you and the woman, and between your seed and her Seed; He shall crush your head, and you shall bruise His heel" (Genesis 3:15).

This proclamation filled Satan with great animosity against Eve. Then, he crafted another plan to permanently destroy man. In this carefully devised second attack against humankind, the enemy fashioned a weapon of eternal condemnation.

This is the spirit of a brutal wolf, to constantly war with the soul *(mind),* and spirit *(heart)* of humankind. This is so that, humankind may become resistant to the saving power of the Seed of the woman *(Jesus Christ)* to be alienated from God *(so that He desist from visiting him and becomes man's enemy).*

The Lord Jesus Christ crushed the head of the serpent by the cross. If that did not happen, it would mean that humankind would perish through his own blood *(by fellow brethren)* without any remedy until no soul lived.

This is the very act of persecuting and killing one another for selfish reasons as it is today amongst those who are captives of the devil. This petitioned autoimmune attack against the human race is still at work until a person is fully born again.

You see your own blood rise up against you. Either within you or through your loved ones. The blood fights you, or you fight others. Just as the ancient beast spoke through the lips of the Jews at the trial of the Lord Jesus before Pontius Pilate and said:

"Let our blood be on us and upon our children" (Matthew 27:25).

When you persecute, falsely accuse or kill another person you condemn your own life to eternal death. Their blood will be required from you and your descendants after you.

Then, your own blood would be demanded from you, because you judged yourself. Once the devil cunningly achieves this against you, it removes love from your spirit; and it plants rage – which is the mark of the beast –*the spirit of a dog.*

Then, you are on your way to the pit of hell where many are captives. Instead of you to be a head and ruler of the earth, there is then a manifestation of an exchange of powers, so that you may become a tail to follow the intents of the devil. Therefore, in that way, the devil has defrauded you.

"Above all, love each other deeply because love covers a multitude of sins" (1 Peter 4:8).

A Gruesome Murder -First Appearance of the Beast

There came a day for Lucifer to implement his evil craft to annihilate man. This time he did not use the serpent. He skilled the wolf and breathed over it his evil breath of envy, and gave it a deceitful friendly character like a serpent.

This was so that, it may hide its evil in its friendly hugs and kisses. Then he sent the wolf to go, and influence Cain with thoughts to kill his brother Abel, and bury him under the ground.

The beast was personally hands on at the tearing of Abel. Abel, the young righteous man who stood sacrificing in the presence of God on the previous day, was on the following day murdered by the wolf of his brother.

I can almost hear Adam telling his wife about a dream which he had seen about the devil coming to attack through Cain. Never make a mistake to think that they did not see these attacks before they happened. They used to see dreams and visions clearly. Surely, Adam did warn Cain as the Proverbs say in these words:

"My son, if sinners entice you, do not consent. If they come and say, "Come with us, let us lie in wait to shed blood; let us lurk secretly for the innocent without cause; let us swallow them alive like Sheol." "My son, do not walk in the way with them, keep your foot from their path; for their feet run to evil, and they make haste to shed blood" (Proverbs 1:11-16).

But like Adam who was tricked so that he did not obey God's commandment not to eat of the fruit, so his son Cain did not obey his instruction, or either that warning from the LORD (Genesis 4:6-7):

And the Lord said to Cain, *"Why are you angry? And why do you look sad and depressed and dejected? If you do well, will you not be accepted? And if you do not do well,* sin crouches at your door; *its desire is for you, but you must master it."*

When all this was happening, the dog was already sitting at the door of Cain's house waiting to befriend him, and to lead him astray. When he went outside it embraced him with a hug and a kiss as one rejoicing over a best friend.

Cain's soul and spirit incapacitated by the power of the energy of the beast taking. It took over his soul to control the rest of his thoughts. Be careful of some hugs.

Cain listened to the blasphemous words of the dog as it slandered Abel, and taught him to be disloyal to God, because He favoured Abel.

Cain strongly possessed by the wolf, followed its instruction to massacre his innocent brother Abel because of his faith in God.

For because of his faith, he offered the best of his produces to God. Beware of friendly enemies who come from outer space to befriend you with intentions to lead you to commit evil that may put you under their life control.

The killing of Abel did not happen without notice. He was not taken by surprise, but it began smoothly with a brotherly outing.

"Cain said to his brother, **"Let us go out to the field"** *(The word field here does not refer to a garden but an arena of entertainment or playground).* **" When they were in the field, Cain rose up against Abel his brother and killed him"** (Genesis 4:8).

How many people are destroyed through such deceitful invitations? A person who carries a spirit of a wolf may initiate a trip or a privy gathering to eat and merry; but along the way they rise to brawl.

Have you ever travelled together with someone or some people somewhere only to return back torn apart and divided, because one of you switched to a beast?

Some women did not come back home after their honeymoon because their husbands became this beast and murdered them.

Some youths also did not come back home after their Christmas outings with their friends, because the beast had marked them for slaughter through their friend/s. Take note of the curse that followed this unpardonable sin, which Cain committed:

"Now you are cursed from the earth, which opened its mouth to receive your brother's blood from your hand. "When you till the ground it shall no longer yield its strength to you" (Genesis 4:12).

The devil wants to see his captives persecute other people for their faith, and righteous deeds, so that in the end their own lives may become unproductive all the days of their lives on earth. He also wants to see their souls banished to eternal condemnation.

The secret of the devil about his spirit of envy is that, the person he targets to destroy is the envious, but not the envied person. When the perpetrator kills the person he envied, he is deceived to think that, he has won the game.

Nevertheless, he is the main target of the devil. After committing the unpardonable sin, the worst follows him all the days of his life, whilst the martyred walks free to heaven.

A fugitive and a vagabond you shall be on the earth (Genesis 4:13).

The vagabond

This was Satan's main final goal against humankind, so that they may become contrary creatures to what God created, and cast away far from Him.

This indeed happens to those who reject Jesus Christ as the only redeemer. However, when they open their hearts to Him, once again the merciful and gracious God turns it around, to rescue them from the cage of the devil.

The pit of Hell and the state of being a fugitive is Satan's final destination forever and ever Amen! He was cast out from heaven to the –underworld. Satan is a fugitive and vagabond without even the keys of Hell his own house. Satan sits under the dominion and authority of Death.

He is without power and authority, and yet, that is where he planned to condemn you. Those who follow at his footsteps also live such as he does in fear of death.

They always fear that they might die wherever they are. Therefore, the devil is always afraid of time as well. Time withdrew from him when the Lord Jesus took the keys of Hell from Him.

Therefore, his mind knows that he does not have time, but limited time. This means that he can no longer be fruitful in completing his schemes and devices.

That is why he is always crying about time. This was the genesis of the mark of the beast, the sign, symbol, and seal of everlasting enmity between Satan and humankind.

Satan is not omnipresent like God. He achieved through the mark of the beast, to make his presence manifest through humans, so that he may daily monitor and pursue them after his fall.

The Lords Jesus spotted the mark of the beast, that animal nature of a dog in man very clearly as He warned:

"I am sending you out like **sheep in the midst of wolves**; *be wary and wise as serpents, and be innocent (harmless, guileless, and without falsity) as doves. [Gen. 3:1.]* **Beware of man;** *for they will deliver you up to councils and flog you in their synagogues,* (Matthew 10:16-17).

You may need to check yourself if you do not have the mark of the beast as Jude writes about some:

"But these men revile (scoff and sneer at) anything they do not happen to be acquainted with and do not understand; and whatever they do understand physically [that which they know by mere instinct], *like irrational beasts–by these they corrupt themselves and are destroyed (perish). Woe to them! For they have run riotously in the way of Cain,"* (Jude 1:10-11).

The lifestyle of a person who has a dog spirit

Unless fully converted to a new creature, you will not know what causes you to persecute your brethren, or to behave evil.

The purpose of breeding a physical dog, and making friends with it, is so that it may bruise anyone who comes to your home without your consent isn't it? That alone says much about your character.

Did you know that most of those who keep dogs have a dog spirit (mark of the beast) in them that causes them to bond with dogs?

Chapter 5

The Evil Power of the Implanted Spirit of the Beast

When contrasting between the powerful anointing that devils dread, and the startling news of the unfortunate precedent evil occurrences to the followers of Jesus Christ, you will see a strange being which is a devil, that stands between the anointed One (Jesus Christ) and the sheep (Soul of man).

This does not shudder at the anointing and presence of God, but it resist and stoutly rebels. A trouble mind would wonder what kind of a devil is this. Disguised with all flashes, this is the wolf/dog, the dread of the shepherd, a predator of the sheep.

It is the inhumane spirit, which Satan implanted in a human being through Cain, the first-born of Adam, the first man on earth.

The Prince of Hell

The spirit of the dog (wolf) has over the past years responsible for the persecution, betrayal, lawlessness, rebellion, shedding of innocent blood, and the slaughter of many of biblical prophets and priests *dating today.* This inhumane spirit can be spotted during prayer, or when communicating with a person.

When you lay your hands on a person to pray for her or him, you must make sure that you discern whether you are facing a demon in a person, or confronting the wolf (man himself).

The same applies when communicating with a person. Many times the spirit of a wolf may be noticed through a language of a person.

Thereby the words of the mouth, you will know what kind of a spirit of a dog his soul is. The kinds of the spirit of a dog/ wolf are all written in the last seven chapters of this book.

The spirit of a dog is not a lower rank demon, but a very higher rank devil, which takes the form of the soul of a person, and becomes a living being –*person or spirit being*.

That is why the old nature of a spirit of the beast in a person is mainly known as a *dog,* instead of saying, '*He is possessed by a spirit of a dog'.*

Although the act of dominating the soul of a human being by the spirit beast is called, possession. Take notice of this phrase from the bible:

"Many dogs have surrounded Me*; strong bulls of Bashan have encircled Me, they gape at Me with their mouths like a raging and roaring lion"* (Psalms 22:12-13).

The dogs mentioned here in this prophecy were the Jews who rose up to rebel against the Spirit of God, afflicted and crucified the Lord Jesus.

Personified by the Beast

This unsuspecting ravenous beast skins between the soul and flesh of a human being who is not born of the Holy Spirit, and Fire. It manifests itself through its wicked activities that are its mark through the thoughts and hands of a person.

The mark of the beast is usually passed on through the bloodline of all humankind. This means that, about 99% of human souls *are born with it.* From the ages of 9 years of child growth upwards, this nature begins to show up.

Dedicate your child to Jesus Christ as early as eight weeks after birth. Let them receive redemption and become new creatures as soon as they turn twelve years, or before the dog spirit begins to manifest and become uncontrollable, leading the child to rebellion.

Sometimes this evil spirit begins to show up very early in the lives of other children, and harass them with its desires. Then you find a little child doing monstrous evil things, which are even far above his age, and thus, the child becomes an abomination.

The spirit of a dog follows a person to mature in his soul even after water baptism. This happens when the Holy Spirit baptism did not happen as a sign of the rebirth.

The rebirth or to be born again converts the soul which was inhumane into a new creature that does no longer conform to the evil spirit of a dog. However, water baptism alone does not transform the soul of a repentant person to a full new creature.

Although he may forsake some acts of sin, but he moves to another act of sin he has never done which relates to the past life of a dog. That is why some Christians have questionable behaviours.

The spirit of dog attends church services

The evil of the dog had been ruling in idol temples, synagogues, and religious temples for thousands of years.

It leads assembles of false religions and has its own people planted strategically in today's churches. These same kinds of people had been a problem in the days of the ministry of Jesus Christ.

They used to stand in the way of those who followed Him and received miracles to charge against them. For several times, they charged Jesus with *'crimes of healing people'.*

The funniest thing is that, they were always in the company of Jesus, followed Him wherever He went, and sat under His teachings in the temple.

Now and again, they threatened to stone Him. The dog follows very close to monitor people so that it may bark and bite.

Even when you take a long road far from dogs, they will pace up to track the smell of the anointing that is upon you. Before you know about it, they will be there behind you. This spirit was crafted by Satan to pursue, and bruise the heels of the "Seed" of the woman.

The shameful thing is that he uses fellow man to pursue man. Indeed a dog does not understand what it is doing. I once attended a revival meeting hosted by a respectable prophet from India. He teaches the truth and he is very radical.

At the closing of the service as he was leading the prayer, I heard a clear sound of howling dogs in one corner inside the building. The people were not wailing, but they were crying like a dog when it senses a negative spirit that may take away their bond master's soul away from them.

This kind of sound of howling has become common in most churches today. The spirit of the dog howls, but the people do not transform from their old self. It is time to cage these evil spirits of the devil, and let the souls of the people of God be loosed?

There is a difference between groaning in the Spirit and the howling spirit of a dog –barking at the Holy Spirit. Discern! The people who have the mark of the beast/ *spirit of a dog* have their own counterfeit spirit that imitates the Holy Spirit.

It has its own manifestations and speaks tongues too. The worse thing with those tongues of the beast is that, they devour and abort breakthroughs.

They hinder true miracles from manifesting in a life of a person by summoning the other principality devils to wage war with the angelic beings of breakthroughs. They bark and bite even after the church service.

Becoming a church member and faithfully attending Bible classes does not guarantee that a person is born again. Neither does receiving healing or any miracle confirms that a person is a true Christian.

Therefore, you will fully know them by their fruits. Not everyone who says to Me, Lord, Lord, will enter the kingdom of heaven, but he who does the will of My Father Who is in heaven" (Matthew 7:20-21).

I have seen highly educated theologians, church members, and fulltime workers of churches who have the mark of the beast.

The spirit of the dog knows how to block ears against the word of God, to hinder people from conviction from sin, so that none may be saved.

And so, are those who attack from within the church. They may be there in the church for years without being convicted by the Gospel, so that they may not be born again at all.

Instead, they sit there watching, or offended by the miracles that follow the Gospel, instigating and scheming against their brethren.

It does not matter to them how clear and anointed your teaching is, they go back to their old ways after church. Meet some of them after church service and ask them,

"How was the service?" And they will tell you that, *"Oh the service was very powerful!"*

However, when you ask more details about what the message was about, you find that, they have forgotten! The amazing thing then, is what was powerful in the church service, if God did not speak anything.

The heart of a person who has the mark of the beast is very hard as a rock. They can make trips to visit all the most powerful men of God in the world, or be under the leadership of a great man of God, but never changed by the word of God. It is not their language as Jesus said to some of the religious people.

"Why do you not understand My speech? Because you are not able to listen to My word. **"You are of your father the devil, and the desires of your father you want to do. He was a murderer from the beginning, and does not stand in truth, because there is no truth in him."**

When he speaks lies, he speaks his own native language, for he is a liar and the father of it" (John 8:43-44).

Church attenders who have the mark of the beast rejoice over receiving miracles now; but they do not maintain a personal relationship with God. They develop familiar spirits and forget where their help comes from.

That is how easy they can destroy a minister within a short time after receiving what they wanted, or for not receiving according to their expectations.

Some of them after giving tithe for several years; they confront their pastors about profits. They give their tithes and offerings with a profit mind-set. The Psalmist cries out to God:

"Malicious and unrighteous witnesses rise up; they ask me of things that I know not. They reward me evil for good to my personal bereavement. But as for me, when they were sick, my clothing was sackcloth; I afflicted myself with fasting, and I prayed with head bowed on my breast and behaved as if grieving for my friend or my brother; I bowed down in sorrow, as one who bewails his mother. But in my stumbling and limping they rejoiced and gathered together against me, and I knew them not; they ceased not to slander and revile me. Like profane mockers at feasts they gnashed at me with their teeth" (Psalm 35:11-16).

When the Holy Spirit is not in a Christian's life, the old nature of the dog takes over them. Apostle Paul in his letters to the Corinthians gives us a clear picture of this. Moreover, the flesh –dog character, dominates the church today.

Very few believers are found walking in the Spirit of God. This affected the ministry of Apostle Paul in Corinth. He had deep revelations and teachings to share with them to take them to higher dimensions in spiritual growth, but their carnal way of doing things hindered him from offloading.

Looking at the time, and the foundational teachings, that he had already taught them, he realised that, there their spiritual growth remained stunted. It shows that there was a dire need for the baptism of the Holy Spirit and fire in Corinth.

"For you are still unspiritual, having the nature of the flesh under the control of ordinary impulses.

For as long as there are envying and jealousy and wrangling and factions among you, are you not unspiritual and of the flesh, behaving yourselves after a human standard and like mere (unchanged) men?" (Corinthians 3:3).

Some Church Leaders Have the Mark of the Beast

Most church elders and some church branch leaders are fully controlled by the mark of the beast. This makes it easy for the devil to scatter the sheep whilst he attacks the Shepherd. This is not a surprise as the early Apostles warned about this for several times.

Apostle Paul said he warned about it for three years. It is very clear that this spirit of a dog looks for opportunities where the church begins to lose focus and begins to become cold. Didn't it wait for the overseer of your church to travel away for another mission as in the case of the apostles?

"I know that after I am gone, ferocious wolves will get in among you, not sparing the flock. Even from among yourselves men will come to the front who by saying perverse (distorted and corrupt) things, will endeavour to draw away the disciples after them," (disciples are believers in Christ) (Acts 20:28-30).

Church leaders who have the mark of the beast have a controlling spirit and envy like Jezebel. They are ever fighting for positions and this hinders spiritual growth of the church.

When they see another member of the congregation grow and functioning with special gifts of the Holy Spirit, they device ways to suppress and frustrate that person.

Others use manipulating powers to cause a person to desert his gift or to use it for himself or herself, but never let the gift to reach far. When invited to preach in churches that have such leaders, you may find it very difficult to preach there.

If they do not tell you what to preach, then they will be sitting by the pulpit with a wristwatch and timing your message. Then they will be signalling to you, *"Time is up, wind up."*

Is this the word of God that you are able to time? Some motivational speeches cleverly composed by the intellect of man, can be timed. In heaven there is no sunrise or sunset, it is always clear daylight.

Nevertheless, we know that, at the camp of the enemy where the spirit of the dog comes from, they always complain that time is short.

This is because, they live in darkness, and their time is short indeed. If truly what you preach in your church is the word of God, why not let Him speak through you until He finishes at His own time.

You refrain from restricting the speech of the kings of this world, but you put time limits and program God's message according to the time on your wristwatch.

It is unfortunate, that you go out to fulfil your worldly deeds with the rest of your limited time. Those are some of deeds of the church leaders, who have the mark of the beast.

Never put people in permanent positions in the church. Some of them as church leaders use their ushering positions to control seats, so that only their friends, relatives, and those who can pay some money may receive the best seats.

Then, there are those who arrange church seating according to class, and best clothing's, whilst the poor seat outside.

"For if a person comes into your congregation whose hands are adorned with gold rings and who is wearing splendid apparel, and also a poor [man] in shabby clothes comes in,

And you pay special attention to the one who wears the splendid clothes and say to him, Sit here in this preferable seat! While you tell the poor [man], "Stand there!" Or, Sit there on the floor at my feet!

Are you not discriminating among your own and becoming critics and judges with wrong motives?

Listen, my beloved brethren: Has not God chosen those who are poor in the eyes of the world to be rich in faith and in their position as believers and to inherit the kingdom which He has promised to those who love Him? But you [in contrast] have insulted (humiliated, dishonoured, and shown your contempt for) the poor. Is it not the rich who domineer over you? Is it not they who drag you into the law courts?" (James 2:2-6).

Before you let anyone establish a branch for your ministry or a home cell, first look at his/her motives behind. Check and test the spirit in that person to see if it is the Holy Spirit or it is the spirit of the dog, otherwise it will one day rise to persecute you. The

Lord Jesus asked the priest, captains of the temple, and elders who came to arrest him,

"Have you come out, against a robber, with swords and clubs? "When I was with you daily in the temple, you did not try to seize Me, but this is your hour, and the power of darkness" (Luke 23:52-53).

Although many say, they are born again because they hold some positions in the church, but they still do not produce relevant fruits. They are coated with the sheepskin, but inside their souls, the wolf has not been cast out.

As a result, they still live like the people of the dark world and become easy sell-outs and targets to the beast –*that ancient devil.* Therefore, they breathe envy against others. They compete, despise their fellow leaders, and plot to destroy them, to the extent of abusing the congregation.

Their services base on financial gains, and material rewards. Apostle Peter sent a warning to the church overseers against some of these practices:

"Tend the flock of God that is your responsibility, not by coercion or constraint, but willingly; not dishonourably motivated by the advantages and profits, but eagerly and cheerfully;

Not domineering over those in your charge, but being examples (patterns and models of Christian living) to the flock (the congregation).

Then, when the Chief Shepherd is revealed, you will win the conqueror's crown of glory" (Peter 5:1-4).

Chapter 6

The Mark of the Beast

The character of Man - 666

He causes all, both small and great, rich and poor, free and slave, to receive a mark on their right hand or on their foreheads, and that no one may buy or sell except one who has the mark or the name of the beast, or the number of his name.

Here is wisdom. Let him who has understanding calculate the number of the beast, for it is the number of a man: His number is 666"" (Revelation 13:16-18).

It has become a common norm for newly born again Christians to talk and warn about stories of the mark of the beast as 666. This made some avoid owning national identity numbers, cell phone numbers, and car number plates that has 666.

Others do not want anything that has to do with items that have number 6 or 999 written on them, because they associate these with Satanism.

However, as some become "old Christians," and get used to church; they forget about their former suspicions on the number 666. Nevertheless, they bounce back to worse practises of the mark of the beast. Therefore, they become the confirmed antichrists as written about in this verse that has 666:

"From that time many of His disciples went back and walked with Him no more" (John 6:66).

The truth is that, they became Antichrists with the mark of the beast. Many people today are no longer walking with the Lord as before.

They have lost the meaning of following Christ. Now their lives are more in the world and doing those things that they once turned their backs on. They are again slandering, they scheme and persecute one another like those who are not born again. Most of today's Christians are full of covetousness, jealousy, and envy.

They walk in competition against one another and they are without peace. Not to mention: A very shameful thing, some have forgotten to read their bibles and to spend time in prayer.

They wake up in the morning to go about their worldly affairs. They do not teach their children to walk in the way of the LORD. Their children are a disgrace without discipline and respect.

E-Commerce and the Mark of the Beast

The Digital age scientists have already developed biometric technologies, which capture the eyes and fingerprints of people, to create their identity files that they use for buying and selling.

Some large organisations have started using this technology on the refuges, and some businesses on their customers.

After shopping, the teal scans the customer's *eyes* to prove identity. Once his financial accounts reflect on the computer, then the customer signs the bill with his *fingerprints.* This may be relevant to the prophesied end times, but it is not what the scripture says here about the mark of the beast:

"He causes all, both small and great, rich and poor, free and slave, to receive a mark on their right hand or on their foreheads, and that no one may buy or sell except one who has the mark or the name of the beast, or the number of his name."

For the whole world to switch to e-commerce where people will use digital codes to shop online and anywhere via machines, then the antichrist will create a means that will cause people to remain where they are, and not to travel to other places to shop or sell.

E-commerce will bring a change of times in the world. Human beings will not be in physical contact with one another in order to buy or sell. However, trade will be via the internet of things, where some coded digits will identify personal information and banking details. In other words, there will be an E-ID.

Although this will mark the full operation of the new last age, which will be termed the *"Digital Age," "Digital World," "One Wold,"* or *"E-Commerce World,"* its main purpose is to facilitate convenient, and smooth self-service trade between seller, service provider, and customer.

As it may seem hassle free, but there is nothing frustrating in the E-Commerce Market places than an unreliable website, slow internet speed, and accounts hacking.

However, wrestling with such difficulties especially in most developing counties, may not be a great deal than the day when the beast will appear to run the E-Commerce Global Markets.

Then, the beast will advance E-Commerce with mandatory means, to force buyers, and traders to implant an E-ID on the forehead, or on their hands. If people are forced to obtain implanted E-IDs so that, they may buy and sell, then, the act of force is the dreaded mark of the beast.

The biggest problem with the implanted E-ID will arise once every soul who has the implant loses privacy. Having one's private information coded in a network embedded chip that is capable to track location may assist with criminal arrests, but may be an irredeemable problem when the beast decides to stalk a particular person for selfish reasons.

For example, there are people who will be at risk of stalking through the implanted chip for exposing the truth about the beast. Another thing, you must know that, although God stays in the secret place, He sees all people under His eye.

However, to learn that there is someone else or some kind of entity that plays 'god' by using the latest technologies to monitor your movement is the most uncomfortable thing and nightmare.

Without doubt, there will be a time where the agents of the beast will just sit down and study people's movements, and their activities through the implanted chips. They will learn from the things they buy through E-Commerce markets, and places they visit.

To fulfil the scripture that's says, *"The world in in the sway of the evil one."* Therefore, there will be a *"New World Order,"* that will govern taxies to a centralised system under the Beast.

In this term, the Beast will be a group of giant nations that will bond together through their leaders to rule the whole world. They will demand what is to be termed, the E-tax. Every soul that buys or sell through the E-Commerce Global Markets will be charged E-tax.

The Spiritual Part of the Mark of the Beast

Now let us return to the spiritual aspect of the mark of the beast, which will generate all the hardships. Take note that the scripture talks about the *right hand and the forehead*. Consider, what kind of mark is this?

Firstly, to mark is to identify with distinct physiognomies that are different from others and thus producing characteristics. A mark therefore is an identified character.

The character of a person is the unseen nature, which. It cannot be described based on the outward appearance of a person. It is a hidden code in the spirit/ heart of a person. Character is what you are when alone and quiet, and revealed when time is ripe *–under pressure*.

"Who among men understands the things of man except by the spirit of man which is in him?" (I Corinthians 2:11).

Prophet Samuel had a little challenge when God sent him to go and anoint another king for Israel instead of Saul.

He went to the right family, but with a physical identity of Saul in mind *–tall handsome man and smooth talking,* but forgot to identify the character.

God who knows the real identity and character of a person whilst he/she is silent or sleeping; He told the prophet:

"Do not look at his appearance or at his physical stature, because I have refused him." "For the LORD does not see as man sees; for man looks at the outward appearance, but the LORD looks at the heart" (1 Samuel 16:7).

Thus said, the mark of the beast represents the state of turning away from the commandments and the love of God and His Son Jesus and thus turning to evil practises.

The First Man with the Mark of the Beast

The mark of the beast remained a hidden code for thousands of years as it is revealed through the case of Cain. Many could not figure out what this is, and where originated.

Anointed ministers from the first disciples of our Lord Jesus Christ defeated the works of Satan through casting out devils, healing the sick perform signs and wonders.

However, many of them suffered attacks and succumbed to death through persecution from those who had the mark of the beast.

Today, thousands of Christians often times suffer persecutions without a cause. The dogs massacred some believers whilst on their knees praying to the Only Living God of all flesh.

Still, nobody could understand or explain the real cause of these killings. The mark of the beast is a long cord traced back to Cain, the first man who was given by God, the mark of the beast.

His act of persecuting and killing his brother Abel distanced him from God. Immediately after killing his brother Abel, Cain lost sense of importance of the existence of God in his life. He lost his human identity and obtained a wolf nature and identity.

That is why Cain arrogantly and defiantly responded thus to God when He asked him about his brother:

"I do not know him." "Am I my brother's keeper?" (Genesis 4:9).

He forgot that, God is omnipresent. He sees everyone, and no person can hid away from His eye.

Moreover, Cain did not know that the blood of humans contains the soul, which identifies the man, and it has a voice that cries to God.

The sense of the presence, knowledge, and fear of God had departed from Cain. Until today, the people who are high ranking under the spirit of the beast like the devil worshipers and atheists deny the existence of God.

"The fool has said in his heart, there is no God, they are corrupt, they have done abominable works, there is none who does what is right" (Psalms 14:1).

After a difficult wrestle with God because of the curses that He laid on Cain: to become a fugitive, and vagabond, Cain propitiated God to consider the safety of his life, lest he dies on the hands of murderers.

He started to fear fellow murderers who were not even there at that period. As mentioned earlier, the fear of death always terrorises the wicked.

However, the righteous are a dread to the evil, as God imparted the children of Israel with awesome to be dreaded.

"This day will I begin to put the dread and fear of you upon the peoples who are under the whole heavens, who shall hear the report of you and shall tremble and be in anguish because of you" (Deuteronomy 2:25).

It is interesting to know according to Genesis 4:16-17 that after Cain went out of the presence of the LORD, he dwelt in the Land of Nod on the east of Eden, and he had established a family with his wife and even had children.

Although the bible writer removed the history about where and how did Cain get a wife?

Nevertheless, God gave him a mark, so that, whoever kills him, vengeance shall be taken on him seven times. This means that, it does not matter how evil a person may be, but you are not given power to kill him/ her. The sin of killing another person is unpardonable, as you have seen it with Cain.

Most of the people, who have the mark of the beast although they are fugitives and vagabonds away from the presence and fear of God, are well established and rich. They have families and children.

They work hard to have enough money to buy guns, pay a hit man and to develop mass destruction weapons for killing the Christians in their worship centres. These are people with cars and houses. They are not physical vagabonds although they are in the spirit realm.

"Then the Lord set a mark on Cain, lest anyone finding him should kill him" (Genesis 4:15).

What kind of mark was this, which could avenge with blood? This was not a dot on the forehead or on the arm of Cain. But, it was the spirit of the beast *(the dog/wolf)* that, initiated him to murder his brother Abel.

Cain displayed the character of a predatory beast. He related with the dog, and guarded by it all the days of his life. Who can face a man who walks with a bulldog?

The wolf devoured and howled at everything that tried to come close to Cain.

Cain and the wolf became one, soul and spirit. This is the dog spoken about in Psalms 22:20. This verse expresses words spoken by the Lamb of God, Jesus Christ when he was going through trial on the hands of the Jews: *"Deliver Me from the sword, my precious life from the power of the dog."*

The dogs confronted and raged against Jesus for more than twelve hours, but He overcame them by resurrecting from the dead. The ancient dog and its power in that war with Christ was with its ten princes of Hell (dogs), to be discussed in the next chapters.

The sin of Adam and Eve brought in sin to the entire human race. Then, the dreadful transgression of Cain laid a heavy burden of condemnation to eternal death, upon all humankind.

The mark of the beast became a generational curse upon all the sons of man. Satan uses this mark to pursue and bruise the heels of those who call upon the name of the LORD, so that man may fall into eternal condemnation and perish by killing one another like wild animals.

Then, what is a dog/ wolf?

In the spiritual context, the 'Wolf' (Dog) is the beast or animal nature in a person, transforming itself *into a hue-man being*. This is the changed aspect of character of human creature, to a strange evil creature. This changes a human being from being the original image of God, to another evil creature:

the image of the beast or son of the devil, instead of elohim or son of God.

This censored natured, not spoken about, is also found in those who have turned away from the grace of God to pursue worldly indulgence and paganism. The wolf possesses a person to become *'the man himself.'* It takes the whole form of the person. Thus, it can speak, think, do, or eat through the body of the person.

"Be not like Cain who [took his nature and got his motivation] from the evil one and slew his brother. And why did he slay him? Because his deeds were wicked and malicious and his brother's were righteous (virtuous)" (1 John 3:12).

What Is the Meaning of 666?

As decoded by the revelation above, in the numeric language 666 is a number of man –representing evil thoughts of the heart and wicked practises of the hands of those who are of the devil –the ancient beast.

You must understand that, in Heaven there is a Lamb of God; but in Hell, there is a wild dog, the prince of Hell. Take note of the difference of the two.

As you continue to read, you will discover that almost 90% of the people of the world have the mark of the beast. Hidden in this code 666 also is the trinity of Satan:

The Ancient Beast

The Beast is the principality of Hell. He is the ancient wolf/dog, which is the evil spirit of rebellion and hostility against God and His Son Jesus.

This ancient beast waged war, had victory over the soul of Cain, and led him to kill his brother Abel. Then, it went, and sat on the right hand of Satan.

It became the supreme power of darkness, which governs the affairs of devils and wizards concerning tormenting, and using souls of man to destroy fellow man.

It ranks next to the serpent that deceived Eve. It is the very evil spirit of Satan, which plants envy and rage. Condemnation is the throne of the Beast established on the heads of its captives.

The beast does not have any pity or mercy on any man, although it rests itself over his soul and works through it. Once it finishes using a person, it vomits him/her out, and wants to see that person dead as soon as possible, like it did to Judas Iscariot.

"Then Judas, His betrayer, seeing that He had been condemned, was remorseful and brought back the thirty pieces of silver to the chief priests and elders, saying, "I have sinned by betraying innocent blood (He repented)" (Matthew 27:3-4).

But take note what the priests said to Judas after

his regret in verse 4: *"What is that to us? You see to it." "Then he threw the coins on the floor and went to kill himself."*

Perdition

This is Hell, the place where devils and their captives will always be found. From perdition arises the Son/s of perdition whose soul is tamed and controlled from Hell, and they live in Hell whilst on earth. Those souls fashioned and controlled by the spirit of the beast in perdition are called *Antichrists*.

There are different ranks of Antichrists and the highest rank is the one who has a voice over the world orders. This is the man from Hell coming from the throne of the beast *–thinks of himself above God.* Like the other Antichrists, he is also born in a body of a human being, with the devil's established headquarters on his mind.

He represents the kingdom of darkness in the world. He speaks instructions of Satan under the power of the beast and full of lawlessness.

From perdition also comes out different spirits of the dogs to impart the Antichrists, so that, they may do different works of darkness, that they are called by the devil to do in the world *(See chapter about the Subterranean Calling)*.

Their main job is to implement evil plans of the beast to: Perpetrate transgression, envy and betrayal, persecute, hinder, pervert, frustrate, control, influence injustices to laws and supports perversion and bloodshed.

"Then Satan entered Judas Iscariot, who was numbered among the twelve" (Matthew 22:3). *"For many deceivers have gone out into the world who do not confess Jesus Christ as coming in the flesh. This is a deceiver and antichrist"* (2 John 7).

Lawlessness/ Anarchy

This is the presence or manifestation of the spirit of Satan, the beast, and the other princes of perdition and wizards. Their evil spirits operate in different forms in the minds and through the hands of those whom they have made captive.

The spirit that carries the practise of lawlessness perpetrates sin, blasphemy, pride, and idolatry. Idolatry operates through the false prophets, or sorcerers. Through the acts of lawlessness, the ancient serpent breathes out the spirit, which empowers the false prophet, so that he may deceive people.

When people are held captive by the deceit of the beast, hell power, and lawlessness, they are bound to manifest the signs of the mark of the beast through their flesh. In this way, they are carried captive down to perdition far from God and His Son Jesus.

When you see these signs of the mark of the beast on a person as explained in Galatians 5:19-20, know that you are dealing with a captive of the devil *–a dog:* Adultery, fornication, uncleanness, lewdness, idolatry, sorcery, hatred, contentions, jealousies, outbursts of wrath, selfish ambitions, dissensions, heresies, envy, murders, drunkenness, revelries, and the like.""

Reject the Mark of the Beast

Whoever has the mark is not born again of the Father, Son (Jesus) and Holy Spirit. I am not talking about attending or joining a particular Sunday church service weekly, because many of those who are found there also have the mark of the beast.

Very few people are truly born again in the churches these days, the rest are wolves in sheep clothing never deciding to repent, and be born again.

"And the smoke of their torment ascends forever and ever; and they have no rest day or night, who worship the beast and his image, and whoever receives the mark of his name" (Revelation 14:11).

To receive the mark of the beast on the hand or forehead means that the person has decided to sell his/her spirit and soul to the devil. This is so that the spirit of the beast may use his/her hands and mind to do anarchy.

The widespread persecutions and massacre of Christians by religious rebel entities and others worldwide is evidence of the manifestation of the mark of the beast placed on their hands.

These are capable to force others to join them in worshiping false gods, but would kill those who confess Jesus Christ as the Saviour, Redeemer, and Son of God.

"They will put you out of the synagogues." All these entities have one purpose as the agenda of the beast *–to purge away all who call upon the name Jesus.* *"And these things they will do to you because they have not known the father nor Me"* (John 16:3). They are not born again! They are antichrists as Jesus said, "*In fact, a time is coming when anyone who kills you will think he is offering a service to God"* (John 16:2).

Chapter 7

The Image of the Beast

To worship the image of the beast has nothing to do with bowing down to a curved or painted image of the beast. However, it simply means to accept and comply with rules and standards of the worldly systems placed by the Antichrist, which are against God's Laws, and against the preaching of the Gospel of Jesus Christ.

"He was granted power to give breath to the image of the beast, that the image of the beast should both speak and cause as many as would not

worship the image of **the beast to be killed"** (Revelation 13:15).

In the recent times, the authorities who have the mark of the beast are forcefully establishing systems for a lawless and rebellious generation of people who are hostile to Jesus Christ. This evil spirits of false worship will advance with intensity in the world to usher in the establishment of the Antichrists rule.

He will be the proclaimer of blasphemous words promoting perversion. The beast will soon release openly its' false prophet who will deceive the world with signs and wonders from the pit of Hell.

The image of the beast is not a statue or designed picture, but a reflection of the beast on those who have taken the mark of the beast. Their character will cause them to turn into the likeness of the beast, even as so proven by the works of their hands. They are sons of the devil.

The son of perdition who is the image of the beast –*Antichrist,* will be revealed to the world. He will impart the world with the breath of rebellion and hostility against God, and the Christ. It is unfortunate that, nations like the Roman Empire, has always bred the Antichrists throughout the bible History when it comes to matters of religion.

Those who betrayed Jesus Christ handed Him to the Romans. They testified that they had no law to judge Him. *"Judge Him according to your own law."* Paul the apostle died still in chains in Rome. There was no justice accorded to him.

The Antichrist authorities that were on power in Rome kept Paul captive. Then, the German nation during the reign of Adolf Hitler manifested the intense presence of the power of the beast against God's people by annihilating many of them.

Yes for rejecting their Messiah Jesus Christ, God gave them up.

History seems to trace its channels to repeat itself with those two nations. There will be a one-world government under ten beasts' nations. They shall reign over them, and will compel people to worship the beast and its mark.

Predictions

Many systems of trade and business will develop to one hub, and all taxes centralized to the beast. Buying and trading will become very difficult for some countries, and business people who will not subscribe to the new economic digital system that will have the mark of the beast.

All people belong to God, and there should not be prejudice in trade based on faith or religion, because that is the mark of the beast.

When that begins to happens, resist. Whether a person is religious or not, that issue must not restrict him from buying, or selling proper things or giving services to potential customers. Daniel describes a vision, which he saw about the beast:

"Thus [the angel] said, the fourth beast shall be a fourth kingdom on earth, which shall be different from all other kingdoms and shall devour the whole earth, tread it down, and break it in pieces and crush it.

And as for the ten horns, out of this kingdom ten kings shall arise; and another shall arise after them, and he shall be different from the former ones, and he shall subdue and put down three kings.

"And he shall speak words against the Most High [God] and shall wear out the saints of the Most High and think to change the time [of sacred feasts and holy days] and the law; and the saints shall be given into his hand for a time, two times, and half a

time [three and one-half years]" (Daniel 7:21-25) [Rev. 13:1-6].

In these trying times, your money will not matter to the agents of the beast, because they will have power to control economies, and ruling systems of strong countries. All products will be enquired to comply with a particular complicated standard, and regulation of the beast, noncompliance no trade.

To be able to export or import their goods beyond their border gates, as even payment modes will be in a form of digital technology exchange. The time is near, and it will be the hard time as Jesus said, "Give Caesar what belongs to the Caesar, and to give God, what belongs to Him." Jesus was referring to taxes. Will the people of this end of the age, *The Digital Age* find it proper, and fair to pay high taxes for trading online?

Converted to the Image of the Beast

The activities of many people already reflect the image of the beast on them. Their evil thoughts and the evil things they practise on daily basis. The law societies work very hard to change the LORD's ordinances on the image of God to fit the image of the beast.

Think about the new passed laws of community support for perversion, and child abortion. Moreover, the religious laws to slaughter Christians, and interdict freedom of worship in the name of Jesus Christ *–all this is the work of the image of the beast.*

"Many shall purify themselves, and make themselves white and be tried, smelted, and refined, but the wicked shall do wickedly. And none of the wicked shall understand, but the teachers and those who are wise shall understand" (Daniel 12:10) [Dan. 11:33-35].

The Antichrists – *Christians Assassins*

There is an evil and radical religion, which is the image of the beast. When you think about a ravenous wolf, then, that is exactly how this religion is. It slaughters the people who do not want to renounce Christianity.

This will be a final trial revenge that, humanity and biblical records has ever recorded. Sorrow that will befall humankind cannot be put at par with the days of the fallen angels, and the flood of Noah.

There will be the highest level of persecutions of Christians by a people whose hearts are as hard as stone.

The scriptures say that the Antichrist will come. The son of perdition will come in the same power of Cain to establish himself soon in the world.

He will sit in the Holy Temple, and proclaim blasphemous things against God and His Son. In other words, he will be found in a church. This Antichrist will deceive the world, in a final trial to win many to hell *(a prison only prepared for devils and Satan).*

"He opposes and exalts himself so proudly and *insolently against and over all that is called God or that is worshiped, [even to his actually] taking his seat in the temple of God, proclaiming that he himself is God"* (2 Thessalonians 2:3-4) Ezek. 28:2; Dan. 11:36, 37; Dan. 7:25; 8:25.

The Antichrists spend a lot of time watching the ways of the Christians to plan snares to block them from prospering in the spreading of the Gospel.

If your ministry is stuck, and you are not moving forward, it could be that, there are rulers of the dark world that hinder your progress. These are Antichrist spirits; they plotted against the Lord Jesus saying,

"You see that you are accomplishing nothing. Look, the world has gone after Him!" (John 12:19).

L y d i a   E ' E l y o n

Types of Antichrists /Front Row Dogs

There are different kinds of antichrist:

1ˢᵗ Type of Antichrists

There are those who deny both the Father and Son and blaspheme the Holy Spirit. These blind enough, they worship any created things including themselves. *"Who is a liar but he who denies that Jesus is the Christ? He is antichrist who denies the Father and Son"* (1 John 2:22)

2ⁿᵈ Type of Antichrists

There are antichrists who believe that there is God in heaven; but they deny that Jesus Christ is the Son of God. These have temples where they have religious meetings to worship God, but teach against Jesus and the resurrection. These too are very dangerous against the Christians, they spare anyone who practises any kind of religious

130

worship, but they kill Christians for their faith in Christ.

"Whoever denies the Son does not have the Father either; he who acknowledges the Son has the Father also" (1 John 2:23).

Apostle Paul was once under this kind of the spirit of the antichrist as he testified:

"Although I was formerly a blasphemer, a persecutor, and an insolent man; but I obtained mercy because I did it ignorantly in unbelief" (1 Timothy 1:13).

3rd Type of Antichrists

There are antichrists that have turned away from the Gospel of truth to false doctrines and satanic deeds for showing power. They enquire from devils.

"They have forsaken the right way and gone astray, following the way of Balaam the son of Boer, who loved the wages of unrighteousness" (2 Peter 2:15). They are empty wells exploiting people by covetousness.

4th Type of Antichrists

There are antichrists who have heard the Gospel, follow it always, but they refuse to be born again, they say, they have not decided to choose Jesus or to be born again. These continue to sin whilst attending church and following great ministers of the Gospel.

"For many deceivers have gone out into the world who do not confess Jesus Christ as coming in the flesh. This is a deceiver and an antichrist" (2 John 7), (see 1 John 3:1-8).

"If anyone who loves the world, the love of the Father is not in him. For all that is in the world –the lust of the flesh, the lust of the eyes, and the pride of life –is not of the Father, but is of the world. And the world is passing away, and the lust of it; but he who does the will of God abides forever" (1 John 2:15).

5th Type of Antichrists

There are antichrists who are rebels who break away from Holy assemblies because of offence to start their own rebel churches.

Rebel churches are all over the world, preaching the gospel of envy and covetousness. The Angel of the LORD returned Hagai the slave of Sarah to go back, and serve her mistress, until she delivered Ishmael.

Division does not come from the Spirit of the Lord Jesus; for He prayed that the saints must be one, as He and the Father are one.

"Anyone who does not love Me will not obey my teaching" (John 14:24).

Unless the Lord has a different assignment, which He desires you to do like He commanded the separation of Paul and Barnabas. There must be a peaceful release of church members to go and pursue the LORD's work. There should not be envious breakaways, led by selfish interest that rises from offence and pride, because that is the spirit of the antichrist.

The rebel churches that mushroom from brake away pastors are all antichrist churches. They are full of earthly dogmata and entertainment programs to keep their blind crowd.

"You have heard that, the Antichrist is coming, even now many Antichrists have come, by which we know that it is the last hour. " They went out from us, but they were not of us; for if they had been of us, they would have continued with us; but they went out that they might be manifest, that none were of us" (1 John 2:18-19).

6th Type of Antichrists

There are antichrists who have sold their souls to the devil for fame and fortune and as objects of snare to the simple. These lead the people of the world into worldly indulgence, lawlessness, and revelry. They are the scoffers of different kinds.

"Scoffers will come in the last days, walking according to their own lusts, and saying, "Where is the promise of His coming? For since the fathers fell asleep, all things continue as they were from the beginning of creations." For this they wilfully forget: that by the word of God the heavens were

of old, and the earth standing out of the water and in the water, by which the world that then existed perished, being flooded by the water. But the heavens and the earth which are now preserved by the same word, are reserved for the day of judgement and perdition of ungodly men" (2 Peter 3:3-9).

These kinds of antichrists will play a major part in this last hour –as it was the days of Noah, entertainment was a daily practise until the flood took them by surprise. At the coming of the Lord Jesus, where will you be? What will your soul and spirit be doing? He is coming like a flood! Yes, like a thief by the night. (Matthew 24:36-44).

The Antichrist Booked for Jerusalem

Now, that very important events have taken place in Israel, we wait for another very important event where Jerusalem is a very important sign of the coming of the Lord Jesus. The City Jerusalem will face war, and there will be destruction of the city that will cause sacrilege. Another nation will rise, whose head of state will be an Antichrist.

He will engage with Israel as though in peaceful terms. However, his entrance and peace agreements with the state of Israel will open a door of iniquity in him. He will place himself in the temple in Jerusalem and proclaim himself god.

"He opposes and exalts himself so proudly and insolently against and over all that is called God or that is worshiped, even to his actually taking his seat in the temple of God, proclaiming that he himself is God" (2 Thessalonians 2:3-4) [Ezek. 28:2; Dan. 11:36, 37; Dan. 7:25; 8:25].

Then, he will command his people to burn Christians on the altar of the temple in Jerusalem. He will do this for a couple of years, and then he will be destroyed.

Chapter 8

The Evil Eye

The mark of the beast is the cause of persecutions, killings, hatred, rivalry, pride, and rebellion. That is why those who have this mark produce wicked fruits. Unless you are born again you definitely have the mark of the beast. More details on the rebirth are in my book: *'The Water of Life'.*

There conditions, characters, and behaviours that confirms a person has a mark of the beast. Below are some signs that you are a captive of the devil with the mark of the beast.

The mark of the beast begins with the evil eye, as Jesus said in a parable,

*"Is it not lawful for me to do what I wish with my own things? **Or is your eye evil because I am good?"*** (Mathew 20:15).

Cain killed Abel for choosing to do what is good with what he had, and for enjoying the proceeds of doing what is good thereafter. God told Cain the similar words because of his evil eye:

"Why are you angry? And why do you look sad and depressed and dejected? If you do well, will you not be accepted? *And if you do not do well, sin crouches at your door; its desire is for you, but you must master it"* (Genesis 4:6-7).

These are some few signs of the mark of the beast, and there are ten different kinds of dogs manifesting these signs, discussed in the following chapters later.

Signs that you have a mark of the beast

1. Sinful inhuman or bestial Anger

2. Condamnation /Suicidal

3. False accuser and slanderer

4. Hypocrite and perjurer

5. Covetousness and Ungratefulness:

6. Sexual Immorality:

Sinful inhuman or bestial Anger

The sinful inhuman or bestial anger results from envy against the success, and prosperity of someone else who is close to you *(your neighbour)*. It leads you to envious jealousy, to covet what you did not work for.

Anger is the father of the devil of pride and rebellion. It is the beast –*the breath of Satan*. *"And Cain was very angry and his countenance fell"* (Genesis 4:5).

Once yielding to this kind of anger tragic sin waves into your spirit to lead you to sinful deeds like –*Satan who coveted the habitation of man; Cain coveted the blessings of Abel; Jezebel coveted Naboth's vineyard; the Pharisees envied Jesus for the multitudes that followed Him.*

There are more acts, including those of women and men who commit adultery with their friend's husbands and wives. All those are signs of the mark of the beast.

The LORD said to Cain, *"Why are you angry? And why has your countenance fallen?" If you do well, will you not be accepted? And if you do not do well, sin lies at your door (the dog). And its jealousy is for you, but you should rule over it"* **Genesis 4:6-7**.

Man was created to rule over all the beasts of the field, but now a spirit of a beast rules him. Notice that this kind of anger knows no mercy or love, it has no peace, and does not relent until it sees bloodshed; a fatal revenge; suffering; or assassination of character of the person angry against. Submit yourself therefore to God.

"Resist the devil, and he will flee from you"" (James 4:7).

Yes! That beast will leave you alone when you resist it. The Lord Jesus instructed His disciples to look for peace wherever they lodge.

"Whatever house you enter, begin by saying, 'Peace to this house.' If a man of peace is there, your peace will rest on him; if not, it will return to you" (Luke 10:5-6).

A place of peace is a place of victory and great growth for your spiritual life. Strife and contention drives away the Holy Spirit. Therefore, you die spiritually, and the devil gains entry to possess you.

"Better is a dry morsel and quietness therewith than a house full of feasting with strife" (Proverbs 17:1).

They may give you good food to eat and expensive gifts, but if they ever quarrel with you for no strong reason what benefit is that stew to you?

You can hardly preach a word with power of God after your spouse has a trifle argument with you under this kind of anger.

A spouse who is a close friend of the devil in this way cannot uplift you, but will surely bring you to zero until you become devil possessed yourself.

Let him or her repent from anger, and be filled by the Holy Spirit, and fire so that, the beast and its mark will go away. Never bark at a barking dog!

When you find yourself in a chaotic discourse with a person leading you into a hot argument; discern who is speaking through him/her. Check whether it is the person talking from the soul realm (natural anger) or from the beast realm.

"Let your conversation be gracious and attractive so that you will have the right response for everyone"(Colossians 4:6).

People who have the mark of the beast speak grieving words, which they regret later. Do not engage in a hot augment with them.

Keep a distance – *"Be wise as serpent and harmless as a dove –do not react but maintain your peace."* If you were in a sound mind, you would not let your tongue loosed to the point of insulting someone.

However, if overpowered by the beast, you become obsessed with darting words of cursing. Those cursing words are the mark of a ravening beast.

"Rather, it is what comes out of a person that defiles them" (Mark 7:15).

Naturally, any person can be angry or frown at wrong or wicked doings.

"LORD, set a guard over my mouth; keep watch over the door of my lips" (Psalms 141:3).

Condemnation

Another sign that you are tormented by the mark of the beast is that, after doing something very bad, you will regret and not even have a proper explanation of why you were overpowered to do that bad thing. Because the beast confiscates love from hearts of people and give them the cold blood of a lizard and the stony heart of a dog.

"But I know you, that you do not have the love of God in you" (John 5:42).

Condemnation is the result of the mark of the beast, and it causes people to condemn themselves for the evil they committed to the point of thinking that they no longer deserve to live. The mark of the beast also uses other people to condemn a person for the wrong, which they have confessed.

Condemnation does not give space for change or repentance. It comes from the devil –*the original sinner who could not repent from his own crimes.* Thus, there is no repentance granted to him for he repents for a while, but returns to his crimes of the ancient rage to kill steal and destroy.

Therefore, those under control of his grip may not be able to do so until they renounce the devil, and receive Jesus Christ as the Lord and saviour of their lives.

"I desire mercy and not sacrifice," that means do not condemn the guiltless" (Matthew 12:7).

After Peter denied Jesus three times, his heart filled with condemnation and grief (Mark 14:7). We thank God for the spiritual umbilical cord that connected his spirit with Jesus Christ, that he cried with great grieve and compassion of the LORD embraced him.

Wherever he was hiding from his shame, the repentant heart connecting him to his maker caused the Holy Spirit to send a message by the women who went to the tomb who witnessed that Jesus is risen –that they may **tell Peter also**, that he has to reunite with his LORD in Galilee (Mark 16:7). Praise the LORD forevermore.

"For if our heart condemns us, God is greater than our heart, and knows all things" (1 John 3:20).

The opposite of condemnation is conviction, love, and forgiveness. If the LORD followed the fishermen of Galilee back in Galilee, and made him His very first fruit of His resurrection to receive the great commission of taking care of the LORD's lambs, and sheep despite all his sins of denying Him in public, then He will follow you too (John 21:15-23).

False Accuser and Slanderer

False accusation and betrayal is another great sign of the mark of the beast. The beast does not shudder at the anointing worse than demons.

In this case, you must remember when they accuse you that, you are dealing with high-ranking devils –*vicious dogs.* They do not understand the language of the Spirit, but they block their ears when He speaks because rebellion is who they are.

The kind of devil serving the beast behind false accusation is called the *Bulldog*. The person, who always rises against you with a bull dog spirit to betray you, is the one who had tested walking very close with you.

Think about the kiss of Judas on the face of Jesus. Although Jesus was not surprised at this, but the spirit of man always wants to know why a fellow human being does such things to a fellow *–it is the mark of the beast so that man may die by his own blood.* The Spirit of the Lord spoke in deep grief:

"If an enemy were insulting me, I could endure it; if a foe were rising against me, I could hide. But it is you, a man like myself, my companion, my close friend, with whom I once enjoyed sweet fellowship at the house of God, as we walked about among the throngs of worshipers" (Psalms 55:12-14).

Therefore, the people who have the mark of the beast use lies as a device of betraying, and persecuting others for the truth. When you teach the truth and walk in truth, this kind of a devil will go behind your heels to throw you in all kinds of tribulations.

To them Truth is the highest degree of crime and abomination. Truth offends them deeply, and they make it controversial by twisting it to a lie to accuse.

Every demonstration of the great power of God offends those who have the mark of the beast. Such things look so strange to them.

You can hardly convince or convict them of sin by the preaching of the Gospel. If they were convicted, then their conversion was for a while, because, they were overcome by the Holy Spirit. Then, you will be shocked when they turn behind your heels to pursue you with false accusation. As the Lord Jesus said,

"Many will be offended, will betray one another, and will hate one another" (Matthew 24:9).

When Apostle Paul stood in a false accusation trial, he had an encounter with higher authorities who had the mark of the beast. They were antichrists, thus, his effort of converting them became an almost result:

Then Agrippa said to Paul, *"You almost convinced me to become a Christian"* (Acts 26:28).

On another case, Stephen a highly anointed disciple of Jesus Christ was falsely accused after preaching Jesus. The Jews killed him for the power of the Holy Spirit, and preaching the Gospel.

They secretly instigated men who said, "We have heard him speak blasphemous words against Moses and God." And they stirred up the people and the elders and the scribes, and they came upon him and seized him and brought him before the council, and they set up false witnesses who said, "This man never ceases to speak words against this holy place and the law," (Acts 6:8-15).

This kind of devil rises within a person's spirit with the ancient hatred against those whose hearts are justified and propelled to worship God.

Even with much evidence of the manifested power of God, this kind of nature of wolf argues against God. *It is capable of resisting the Spirit of God and the anointing.* Above all, the Lord Jesus encouraged His disciples so that they may overcome it from within their spirits:

"Blessed are you when men hate you, and when they exclude you, and revile you, and cast out your name as evil, for the Son of Man's sake. Rejoice in that day and leap for joy! For indeed your reward is great in heaven, for in the like manner their fathers did to the prophets" (Luke 6:22-23).

Hypocrite and Perjurer

"For they preach, but do not practise, they tie up heavy burdens, hard to bear, and lay them on people's shoulders, but they themselves are not willing to move them with a finger. They do all their deeds to be seen by others, for they make their phylacteries broad and their fringes long" (Matthew 23:2-5).

Hypocrisy is a sign of the mark of the beast. Most of the people who practise hypocrisy are very religious and critical about other people who do not follow what they follow –*traditions and customs*. In Matthew 23 verses 1-36, the Lord Jesus scolded the Pharisees, because of their hypocrisy:

*"**Woe to you, scribes and Pharisees, hypocrites!** For you build the tombs of the prophets and decorate the monuments of the righteous saying; "'If we had lived in the days of our fathers, we would not have taken part with them in shedding the blood of the prophets.' **Thus, you witness against yourselves***

that you are sons of those who murdered the prophets. *Fill up, then, the measure of your fathers"*(Matthew 23: 29-33).

Covetousness and Ungratefulness

Covetousness is another sign of the mark of the beast. It springs out greed and inordinate desire often for another person's possessions.

This spirit causes people not to be content with what they have, but look for means how to get what belongs to someone else.

You do not want to see a good thing on the hands of someone else, instead of rejoicing you feel angry that they have something.

Those who are covetous demand people to take off their clothes from the body and give it to them. Are you building a new house? They will develop strategies how they must take it or stop it from finishing.

This is the sign of a mark of the beast. Covetousness works with witchcraft. I have observed many churchgoers who have this sign of a mark of the beast. When severe, it leads to persecution and killing.

When you buy a new car, they come and walk around it to see if it is better than theirs is, and they would be investigating among themselves; *"Where did she get it?" "How much is it?"*

"Woe to those who devise iniquity and work out evil upon their beds! When the morning is light, they perform and practice it because it is in their power. "They covet fields and seize them, and houses and take them away; they oppress and crush a man and his house, a man and his inheritance" (Micah 2:1-2).

Many people have a collection of things that they coveted and grabbed from other people. One day I was wearing a pair of nice new shoes, someone decided to tell me that she want the same shoes.

Knowing the kind of spirit that she had, I decided to give them and I remained with none. One day she saw me dressed in a nice jacket, and she demanded that, she wanted the same jacket. I removed it from my body and gave it to her, but she was almost angry because it did not fit her at all.

In all this, I was observing what manner of spirit is this, which also overtakes fulltime church people. I looked at a church elder who grabbed a new study bible from a ten-year-old boy, and she exchanged it with her old bible. Doesn't a child need a good bible?

In 2006, when I had just worked for only two years, I received a phone call from a woman who instructed me to go and make a loan at the bank so that her daughter may buy a car.

She said that her husband does not want to drive her to work with his car. Meanwhile, I did not even have a bicycle myself. When I declined her request, she began to behave funny and angry.

This mark of the beast has caused many women to think highly of themselves, that good things must come to their houses and to their own sons and daughters, but not to someone else's children. So that they may prove a point and showoff. The LORD strongly warns against covetousness.

"You shall not covet your neighbor's house, your neighbor's wife, or his manservant, or his maidservant, or his ox, or his donkey, or anything that is your neighbor's" (Exodus 20:17) [Luke 12:15; Col. 3:5].

Covetousness is sure animalism. It is a mark of a dog that can easily reduce your life span. People of this nature never at any point have peace because contentment is not in them.

"You are jealous and covet what others have and your desires go unfulfilled; so you become murderers. [To hate is to murder as far as your hearts are concerned.] You burn with envy and anger and are not able to obtain the gratification, the contentment, and the happiness that you seek, so you fight and war. You do not have, because you do not ask" (James 4:2) (1 John 3:15).

Sexual Immorality

Promiscuity and sexual lust is a mark of the beast. The act of having sex with just about anyone is certainly the manifestation of the mark of the beast.

What follows that evil spirit are: setbacks, limitations, regrets, broken marriages, failures, parent less children, sexual transmitted diseases and poverty.

The kind of the devil responsible for the spirit of lust is called the *Street dog*.

This devil has caused much havoc in people's everyday lives, including the Christians. Those possessed by this spirit do not have any sense of shame or guilt for the evil things they do.

Chapter 9

The Serpent and the Dog

The evil works of the instigator

The instigator operates through both a spirit of a fearful *hunting dog* and the serpent. These spirits cause their captives to be threatened by the presence, or success of another. Instigators are very proud and haughty people who domineer through pulling down others by the coiling serpent *–a python spirit.*

A person who is possessed by the demon of instigation is always afraid to confront another person over an issue. However, he/she goes at the back of that person to instigate him/her to another repeatedly, until a wicked scheme is fashioned against the instigated person.

These two evil spirits, the serpent and the fearful hunting dog are most common in women than in men. This is what causes women to despise others with great contempt, to reproach, gossip and instigate other people. They manifest the things that the Lord hates:

"A proud look [the spirit that makes one overestimates himself and underestimates others], *a lying tongue, and hands that shed innocent blood,* (Ps. 120:2, and 3).

"A heart that manufactures wicked thoughts and plans; feet that are swift in running to evil" (Proverbs 6:17-18).

Jezebel instigated in order to forcefully get Naboth's vineyard. Make a careful study of this instigation, and check yourself if you are not like that, or something like this has ever happened in your life:

Jezebel's instigation

"Jezebel his wife said to him. Do you not govern Israel? Arise, eat food, and let your heart be happy. I will give you the vineyard of Naboth the Jezreelite. Therefore, she wrote letters in Ahab's name, and sealed them with his seal and sent them to the elders and nobles who dwelt with Naboth in his city. Moreover, in the letters she said,

"Proclaim a fast and set Naboth up high among the people. And set two men, base fellows, before him, and let them bear witness against him, saying", *"You cursed and renounced God and the king. Then carry him out and stone him to death."*

Moreover, the men of his city, the elders and the nobles who dwelt there, did as Jezebel had directed in the letters sent them.

They proclaimed a fast and set Naboth on high

among the people. Two base fellows came in and sat opposite him and they charged Naboth before the people, saying, Naboth cursed and renounced God and the king. Then, he was carried out of the city, and stoned to death (1 Kings 21:7-13, 19).

The Evil Force of Instigation

This spirit of a fearful hunting dog pushes people to act more superior over others. A discerning man cried out:

"Lord, MY heart is not haughty, nor my eyes lofty; neither do I exercise myself in matters too great or in things too wonderful for me" (Psalm 131:1).

As in the character of Balak, the king of Moab, a fearful hunting dog spirit always depends on the power of a snake spirit. They look for a serpentine person to assist them in cursing the blessed and prosperous one. However, they always fail to obtain what they wanted, even though it had cost those fortunes.

"Pride goes before destruction, and a haughty spirit before a fall" (Proverbs 16:18).

Balak employed Balaam to go and curse the children of Israel, because he saw greatness and might in them, and he was afraid that, they might take over his kingdom. They did not fight him in anyway, and yet he began to feel intimidated.

There are people like this, who have this spirit of a fearful dog. They begin to feel uneasy when they see a new comer. They feel threatened that, this new person will take their job positions from them, or they are uncomfortable by your building in their area, and they rise up to instigate.

"Now come, I beg of you, curse this people for me, for they are too powerful for me. Perhaps I may be able to defeat them and drive them out of the land, for I know that he whom you bless is blessed, and

he whom you curse is cursed" (Numbers 22:6).

The Coiling and Squeezing Serpentine Spirit

The evil spirit that was in Balaam is a two-headed serpent operating in most soothsayers and false prophets. Because of money and love for material gifts, many pastors and spiritual people stand in the position of Balaam.

They do not admonition a sinner who falsely accuse, but they take sides with him/her. They give their ear to instigation meant to manipulate them, so that they may declare curses over the lives of those opposed by their followers. This very thing is what the Lord warned against in the churches.

"Nevertheless, I have a few things against you: you have some people there who are clinging to the teaching of Balaam, who taught Balak to set a trap and a stumbling block before the sons of Israel" (Revelation 2:14).

You find a pastor getting involved in issues that does not concern him. Before even investigating the truth, he pronounces curses over the other person who instigated. A member, soon after bringing the tithe, keeps coming back to the pastor's house to instigate another member of the church.

The pastor passes demonic verdicts without even bringing in the accused person to hear the matter from both sides. Instigators offer appealing things to people, so that they may pronounce curses over those who intimidate them.

They go about complaining in their gossip:

"Do you think it is right that this fellow be that, do that or be given that?" "They have done this... and that and I am sure they want to take my position."

Discern and do not answer to her instigation. When you advise otherwise in a manner, which does not favor the instigator, you see her go to someone else to instigate you. You become her target:

"Do you think that it is right that so 'so apprises my rival who threatens my position?"

The practices of the serpentine spirit have dominated most churches. Remember that the spirit of the serpent and the dog are ancient evil spirits, which war against souls of humankind. These evil spirits as princes of Hell work together.

It is always sad to see a man of God enticing these evil spirits by cursing their fellow, just to gain favor from the wicked accusers. Some Pastors do not mind standing on their pulpits, which they dedicated to God, and they speak curses against another man of God.

Know the source of their influence! The Holy Spirit gives concern and compassion towards your fellow brethren, but not hatred and rage based on heresy and rumors.

"You shall not revile God [the judges as His agents]
or esteem lightly or curse a ruler of your people"
(Exodus 22:28).

A squeezed prophet in South Africa

A particular young prophet in South Africa travelled from his area to another part of his country and established a big tent meeting, with hundreds gathering. A few moments later, he wittingly went to the community radio station and announced with excitement:

"The Lord has sent me as a prophet to this area, because there is no prophet here." Now, the listeners heard that, he said God said there is no prophet in their area. They phoned one another, and their phone calls went through the Balaam's of that area. So, those who thought of themselves as prophets rose up against the young prophet: "What does he mean by saying that there is no prophet in

this area, because we are here"?

They gathered all their fellows, fasted and prayed against the prophet. The spirit of the serpent was invoked to squeeze out all the living waters from the young prophet. Then within a few months, his church became empty and those pastors who cursed him remained to laugh about it until today –mocking the empty tent.

"Therefore His people return here, and waters of a full cup are drained by them" (Psalm 73:11).

Therefore, a few years later that whole area became very dry. However, after their incident, the land suffered shortage supply of water, until scarcity of water became a common problem in the area.

Most of their water sources became dry, animals and people suffered to the point that the media was invited to come and broadcast the news about their drought.

The sad part is that broadcasting problems on media may not produce water, but attention. However, when a people humble themselves, repent from sin, and pray to God; He hears from heaven and sends healing to the land.

Pastors entertain the spirit of instigators

It is unfortunate that the church has opened doors to the python and the spirit of the wolf to curse the saints of God. These two evil spirits run many churches today, but the Holy Spirit is reject.

One needs to discern first, to know which church to set your foot to, or which prayer meeting to join. Even some of the friends you make in the church, you must clearly know what spirit is in them, before you find yourself drained by the coiling serpent, and bitten by the dog's spirit, which might be upon them. Remember how Abel was killed by his own brother.

The Instigated Pastor

People make the mistake of forgetting that, the cellphone has *'screenshot* 'and *'send buttons.'* It is very disappointing to learn that, the person you thought is good supports instigations against you.

Another pastor spoke insolent, and curses against me with her *"spiritual daughter."* Below is their conversation, which I captured without their awareness, and I kept it as evident record until today.

Pastor: *"My daughter, remove this thing from there before the end of this week or it will die."*

The woman responded, *"Yes daddy I will tell her to go,"*

The pastor responded, "*Yes, I no longer want to hear that this thing is still there, otherwise you must buy a coffin."*

The woman laughed, "*Kkkkkkk! Yes, daddy I know*

you, and I have seen your power fighting 'so 'n so' (Name withheld, they mentioned her big boss at work, whom I also knew).

What kind of Power was that?

There is nothing spoken against the righteous in secret which God does not reveal to them. I captured this conversation as it is, and I kept it somewhere without even showing, that I already know that they were referring to me as *"this thing"* and had declared a coffin over my life.

"Curse not the king, no, not even in your thoughts, and curse not the rich in your bedchamber, for a bird of the air will carry the voice, and a winged creature will tell the matter" (Ecclesiastes 10:20).

You are commanded to bless, but not to curse. God has commanded a curse upon those who curse His people, and a blessing upon those who bless them, and that's all. Curse, and you will be accursed by

God; bless, and you be blessed. It is a heavenly principle.

Chapter 10

Beware of Dogs

Now that you have already acquired much knowledge about the power of the dog, surely you have understanding about the nature of a human being.

In the following chapters, you will learn about the higher levels of the dominions and kinds of powers of the dog, which lives in real people.

Therefore, you must understand that, whatever kind of character you will identify with any person from any of the kinds of dogs discussed here is of the devil, and is contrary to the image of God.

This chapter is an introduction of the next ten chapters, which exposes the kinds of power of a dog in details. It is unfortunate that these evil entities do not move and live successfully in their misty beings, but they always look for a human being to ride on.

As a result, people look at each other as evil and wicked and yet the real evil is walloping somewhere within the human body.

The person himself or herself who is under the control of the power of a dog may not know it. Because it is the spirit of a dog, but not his own will that overrule him, until he is born again.

The world has evil rulers, powers, principalities and initiators from the dark world which stand to overshadow the earthly rulers. Moreover, most of these personify themselves through real people. They live, move and have their beings in people.

"I will not talk with you much more, for the prince (evil genius, ruler) of the world is coming. And he has no claim on Me" (John 14:30).

The Subterranean / Wicked Calling

Unlike the Angels of the LORD, who are responsible for particular heavenly assignments in the lives of people, called by God, these are infernal spirits.

They work with hosts of demons who kill, destroy, and pull people into darkness. They operate through human beings.

Those who have an evil calling by Satan, and bestowed with these powers, are referred to as *the captives of the devil* or the possessed. Those whom they attack, or oppose are termed as, *'the oppressed or persecuted'.*

Those called by Satan, and anointed with the evil powers of the dog manifest their underworld works in the world through the terrestrial domain doors. These are the secular activities of people, which portray their dominion, strength, and power in the world.

They forsake God's ordinances, and they do not inquire of His will, as it was in the days of Noah. The evil rulers, powers, principalities and initiators in the infernal or underworld of darkness, manoeuvre in the physical world through human beings of different ranks, classes and levels of influence.

They pervert every unborn again soul, living in it unless he/she sought Jesus Christ the redeemer. They take the whole form of the human embodiments, soul and body, to become spirit beings imparting a dog or wolf (beast) nature in the soul.

Demons submit under these rulers, principalities, powers as initiators to fulfil special assignments through people, whilst they sit behind and masquerade their identity.

These masters of the demons cause rebellion and oppression among people. Do not be ignorant nor turn a blind eye. In this world, there are those who daily called, and anointed by devils.

They are then deployed with unclean spirits to carry out wicked missions somewhere in almost all the terrestrial domains of people like: Royal palaces, business centers, cities, hospitals, schools, social clubs, synagogues or churches, malls, science and technology places media houses, sports centers, transport business, shops, houses, homes, markets and hotels.

"In the dark they break into houses which they have marked for themselves in the daytime; they do not know the light. For the morning is the same to them as the shadow of death; if someone recognizes them, they are in the terrors of the shadows of death"(Job 23:16-17).

This revelation will enlighten you about the world, which the Lord Jesus mentioned to God in His prayer, when He prayed for all the saints:

"I have given them your word and **the world has hated them; for they are not of the world,** *just as I am not of the world. I am not asking that you take them out of the world, but that you* **keep them from the evil one"** *(John 17 :14-15).*

It is your responsibility as a true Christian, to pull out from the hand of the enemy, those who have this wicked calling. Remember that we do not wrestle against flesh and blood, but against these powers and principalities in the cosmic spheres. The Lord Jesus told Nicodemus:

"God did not send his Son into the world for Him to judge the world. *This means that He was not sent to judge it unpleasantly, condemning all humans to destruction. Rather, as Jesus says,* **he was sent "for the world to be saved through Him"** *(John 3 :17).*

When the time for the Lord Jesus had fully come to redeem and save all men from sin and transgression, these same ten powers (dogs/wolves) were in the forefront humiliating, howling, and tearing the Him.

Yes, the spirit of a righteous man is harmless as a dove. Through the mouth of David, the Lord spoke about the oncoming attack by the dogs that were to kill him.

"For dogs have compassed Me: the assembly of the wicked have enclosed Me: they pierced my hands and my feet. I may tell all my bones: they look and stare upon me. They part my garments among them, and cast lots upon my vesture. But be not far from me, O Lord: O my strength, haste for you to help me. Deliver my soul from the sword; My Soul from the power of the dog"* (Psalms 22:16-2).

This verse here gives a graphic picture of what happens when dogs attack a person. Take notice that, a wolf/dog is one of inferior beasts in the earthly realm. Yet, it is of superior rank in the evil spirit world.

Spiritually, dogs are almost in every realm, to purport cosmic evil agendas. These are the unclean devils usually called, *strongman, principalities, or powers*. An example is this one found in the book of Mark:

'As soon as Jesus got out of the boat, **a man with an unclean spirit came from the tombs"** (Mark 5:2-3).

A dog/wolf is the heckler and evil ruler; power; principality; and rebel beast in the spirit realm. It does not want to be known as a dog though.

When it manifests itself in the spirit, it disguises itself as a very big monster, a person, or a big name just to cause dread. For example, a Lion, leopard, tiger, elephant, crocodile, a fictional monster that does not even exist, or the man next door.

Yes, a dog does see itself as the owner of the body that it lives in. When confronted by the spirit of a dog in person, it usually says, *"You mean who, me?"*

You must learn to discern all your battles, and kinds of enemies. Check what exactly are you fighting with, or fighting for? When Gideon was going for war against the Midianites, the LORD God gave him a sign of 300 dogs, to tell him what kind of army of the enemy he was going to fight with *the Median spirit of a dog.*

"Then the LORD said to Gideon ; 'With the three hundred men who lapped the water like dogs, I will save you and deliver the Midianites into your hands. But all the others are to go home" (Judges 7:7).

Know the power of the Rock of Ages against dogs. But, Goliath thinking he will deter the mind of David said:

"Am I a dog that you come to me with sticks?" (1 Samuel 17:43).

Nevertheless, David had seen correctly, there was a spirit of a dog in that Goliath's body. Yes, of course little dogs are afraid of sticks. Therefore, he took stones also to overcome it by killing Goliath.

"For you shall be in league with the stones of the field, and the beasts of the field shall be at peace with you" (Job 5:23).

David challenged and killed Goliath with one stone in the name of the LORD; because he had a revelation about the kind of spirit, he was confronting. In real life, when you see a dog, just bend down, and pick a stone against it, and you will see it move backwards, and disappears.

Jesus triumphed over the powers of the dog and of the serpent, crushing even its head on Golgotha. He proclaimed:

"*It is finished!*" (See John 19:28-30.)

That became the end of the power of the Dog. Without knowing the truth you can find yourself bound by the defeated antagonist. Beware of dogs!

Caution!

As you read the following sensitive chapters, be full of compassion for all humanity, and do not pass your final judgment on anyone through whom you have spotted the things you read. Therefore, apply the priestly procedure, remembering that you were also once like that (Ephesian 2:1-6).

Chapter 11

Beware of the Wild Dog Spirit

T he wild dog is the chief prince of Hell, or the *son of Lucifer.* It the evil spirit, that was born of his rage. It is the cause of rage, rebellion, and tumult all over the world. This is the ancient wolf, which is the devil who is the murderer.

It is the same beast, which had its mark on Cain. The Lord Jesus spoke about this kind of a devil for the first time in details, but surely, the people did not understand what He was telling them about.

"You are of your father, the devil, and it is your will to practice the lusts and gratify the desires [which are characteristic] of your father. **He was a murderer from the beginning** *and* **does not stand**

in the truth, because there is no truth in him. When he speaks a falsehood, he speaks what is natural to him, for he is a liar [himself] *and the father of lies and of all that is false"* (John 8:44).

The Brood of the Viper

The wild dog/ wolf, has power over thousands of devils of its kind (dogs) and of different ranks. It also heads the rest of the nine (9) arch devils (spirits of dogs) appointed by Satan to pursue, monitor, and persecute human beings, especially those who are redeemed by the Blood of the Lamb of God – Jesus Christ of Nazareth, the Son of God.

"Then I saw the beast and the rulers and leaders of the earth with their troops mustered to go into battle and make war against Him Who is mounted on the horse and against His troops" (Revelation 19:19).

These also have thousands of subject demons of their kind under them. The wild dog is a beast, which ranks in power next to the serpent, which tempted Eve in the Garden of Eden.

This is the brood of the viper, who is the only son of Lucifer and the ancient dragon. It sits on the right hand of Satan as a prince and power of Hell and it is responsible for idol worship. This is where the power of a dog mentioned in Psalms 22 originates:

"Deliver my life from the sword, my dear life from **the power of the dog"** (Psalm 22:20).

This spirit of a dog fights against repentance, and forgiveness of sin. It promotes rebellion, lawlessness, and false religions. It has power over all pagan worship. The people used by the wild dog spirit lead false worship (idolatry) gatherings.

It imparts its captives with the power to shed the blood of innocent souls –*and that becomes their strength*. You must understand that the devil does not have power; he depends on the blood of human beings and animals to energise himself.

The wild dog is the overall ruler/master of darkness in the spiritual and physical world where it manifests itself through human beings.

This unclean spirit mainly possesses, and uses those who are in high positions of influence and leadership of people for example: Queens, kings, politicians, governors, presidents, teachers, rulers, priests, religious leaders, group masters, and all other high-ranking leaders. Even with the highest level of education, the spirit of this wolf knows no diplomacy.

"Yea, they are greedy dogs which can never have enough" (Isaiah 56:11).

Have you not seen members of the parliament or politicians howling and grinning at each other in the 'Honourable house'? In the campaign for elections, many fight their ways to the top by lies, slandering and tearing others. The spirit of the wild dog causes that.

This kind of a devil gives most leaders the power to influence the laws with irresistible customs, teachings, traditions, and religious beliefs to try to frustrate, and pervert the ways and laws of God.

Biblical examples of people who were possessed and used by this kind of devil, the wild dog spirit, are: Pharaoh, Jezebel, Queen Athaliah, Jeroboam, Nebuchadnezzar, Aaron *(fell into the temptation)*, and then all the Kings who were named –Herod, were possessed by the wild dog devil.

They operate in dual forms, both as human beings, and as spiritual entities in the high places. Daniel personally experienced a vivid dramatic manifestation of this wild dog spirit.

*"But for twenty-one days **the spirit prince of the kingdom of Persia blocked my way.** Then Michael, one of the archangels, came to help me, and I left him there with the spirit prince of the kingdom of Persia"* (Daniel 10:13).

This was the wild dog evil spirit operating through the king of Persia. Wild dogs work behind the scenes. Their subjects dread them; none reveals their evil secrets easily. The Syrian king was uncomfortable when he heard that: *"Elisha the prophet, who lives in Israel, tells the king of Israel what you talk about in your bedroom!"* (2 Kings 6:12).

Those who have this wicked calling to serve this unclean spirit do not fear any man of God. They do not shudder at the word of God nor respect the anointing. The stronghold possessing power of the wild dog hold people's minds, so they cannot think otherwise as clearly stated by Apostle Paul to the Corinthians:

"The god of this age has blinded the minds of unbelievers, so that they do not see light of glory of the gospel of Jesus Christ, who is the image of God. Their minds are veiled lest the light shines on them and they are saved from perishing" (2 Corinthians 4:4).

Under the dicing veil of the wild dog spirit, there is cynicism and a very heavy cloud of darkness that causes captives to repent but for a while. Here is an example of an incidence from the book of Acts where Apostle Paul had an encounter: Then Agrippa said to Paul,

'Can you persuade me in such a short time to become a Christian?' (Acts 26:28).

Above all this, the wicked ways of this devil possessed people are vain before the presence of the LORD God. They may feel highly elevated in power when they walk on earth, because they can load it over people, they growl and bite. Nevertheless, when the most awesome presence of God comes down,

"He takes away the understanding of the chiefs of the people of the world, and they wander in desert wastelands. They grope in the dark without light, and He makes them stagger like a drunken man" (Job 12:24-25).

Chapter 12

Beware of the Bulldog Power

The bulldog is a principality territory controlling devil. It operates as the military commander of Hell especially in the physical realm. It works as a servant on behalf of those in the underworld. It is subject to a wild dog who may be a principality in the real world or in the spiritual realm.

These are commanders or second in authority over the pack of wolves/dogs in the army of the defeated kingdom of darkness.

It possesses people who work in the military, and some people who have a soldier like spirit of fighting. It causes the possessed to intimidate people, and to fight wrong battles for the purpose of destruction.

Many people under the control of this evil spirit have evil powers as evil soldiers. Their power is to betray, rebel, conspire, falsely accuse, intimidate, condemn to trial, hardship, persecution, and massacre or murder.

These also fight to overthrow rulers/powers, so they lead their people in disarray. Here is an example:

Then Abishai the son of Zeruiah said to the king, *"Why should this dead dog curse my lord the king? Let me go over now and cut off his head"* (2 Samuel 16:9).

That is the spirit of a bulldog right there. They also form criminals of war, genocide attacks, and violence leading riots and rebellious protests. Here is another example:

Accordingly, Judas came to the garden, guiding a detachment of soldiers and some officials from the chief priests and the Pharisees. They were carrying torches, lanterns and weapons (John 18:3).

This unclean spirit also operates more in places where there are gatherings of people who meet daily on common grounds like schools, hostels, sports arenas, rallies and mass gatherings. In schools, it uses some children to torture pupils, until they develop a very low self-esteem.

It causes children to disobey parents and the elderly also. This same evil spirit was upon Haman the enemy of the Jews. It was influencing him to harass and plan to annihilate the Jews, to the extent that he begged for authority from the king to kill them:

"So the king removed the signet ring from his finger and gave it to Haman son of Hammedatha, the Agagite, and the enemy of the Jews" (Esther 3:9-10).

After the Jews charged Jesus with treason, this kind of devil that was upon the soldiers to derision, and bully him as recorded:

"Many bulls have surrounded me; strong bulls of Bashan have hedged me in [Ezek. 39:18]. For dogs they have encompassed me; a company of evildoers has encircled me, they pierced my hands and my feet" (Psalm 22: 12, 16) [Isa. 53:7; John 19:37.].

Now, exactly as it was written in the scriptures, Matthew 27:27 records how the soldiers bullied the Lord Jesus all the way to where they crucified Him. But, He arose in victory! The very bulldogs were confounded, and put to shame.

Chapter 13

Beware of the Guard Dog

The guard dog is third in rank of the unclean spirits of the underworld. It is responsible over the gates and premises of hell. It guards against any works of righteousness that disturbs the evil activities of Satan and his devils. Its purpose is to please rulers, powers, and dominions in the earth and spirit realm.

These are evil and unclean securities/ evil watchers/ monitors appearing as black dogs in the spirit realm. Guard dogs have masters who give them commands and orders when deployed.

When you see a black dog in your dream, it means that there is an evil person who has the power of a guard dog assigned by the ark devil to monitor you, and performs wickedness against your life behind your back.

This evil spirit also works with fellow evil spirits in a very large troop with one mind. They are taught how to keep secrets. They never tell the truth, but lies.

They also influence bandits in the physical realm to lay snares against the gospel, and they kill everyone who promotes righteousness through Jesus Christ. They guarded the tomb of the Lord Jesus with an evil purpose as assigned by their masters.

"After the chief priests had met with the elders and formed a plan, they gave the guards a large sum of money and instructed them: You are to say, His disciples came by night and stole Him away while we were asleep" (Matthew 28:12).

The captives of the devil who had this same guard dog spirit also monitored Daniel to make sure, that he did not pray to his God *(Daniel chapter 3)*. After realising that, Elisha the prophet was able to hear and see what is happening in their houses without being there, the king of Syria sent people to go, investigate and monitor Prophet Elisha, so that, he may send bulldogs to attack him:

"Go, find out where he is;" the king ordered, *"So I can send men and capture him."* The report came back: *"He is in Dothan."* Then, he sent horses and chariots and a strong force there. **They went by night and surrounded the city** (2 Kings 6:11-16).

People who are possessed by the guard dog make a careful follow up and watch to monitor all your activities to destroy the works of your hands before it is established.

They stalk you without you knowing about it, and they try to strike without notice. Be consistent in your prayer because you do not know the evil day. Moreover, pray for your deliverance if you have this evil calling.

That evil spirit, which causes you to sleep when you are supposed to watch and pray, is the same spirit of the guard dog. Most unfortunately, all those troops who were sent were stricken with blindness just on arrival. They could not do anything to harm Elisha, his property, and his servants.

"Do not fear, for those who are with us are more than those who are with them" (2 Kings 6:16).

The kingdom of darkness does not have the capacity to produce more devils to protect their captives.

Chapter 14

Beware of the Hunting Dog Force

The hunting dog is a stubborn ravenous, cold-blooded Antichrist predatory force of darkness. This unclean spirit possesses people so that they may become evil strike forces. It causes people to brutally shed blood, scheme to grieve emotionally and destroy spiritually.

They also influence the spirit of pride and rebellion. Most of those possessed and used by the evil hunting dog spirit are ritual murderers, kidnappers, robbers, instigators, backhanders, scammers, fraudsters, human traffickers, slave traders, evil diviners, sorcerers, slanderers, soothsayers, devil worshipers, Satanists, occult leaders, black and white witches, magicians, and wizards just to mention few.

The practise of consulting witchdoctors and soothsayers comes from this kind of a spirit of a dog. King Saul after he was left by the Holy Spirit, he became possessed by this unclean kind of spirit of a hunting dog. As a result, he pursued to kill David. One day he killed a priest of God who showed kindness to David by giving him bread and the sword of Goliath.

"Then king Saul ordered his henchmen, Surround and kill the priest of God" (1 Samuel 22:17).

How many people of God did someone's henchmen kill? Now, the other Saul who later converted to a believer in Christ Jesus changed his name to Paul. This was to break away from ties with his family roots, which had this hunting dog spirit running in their bloodline. He was also a Benjamite, the same tribe of king Saul.

"Benjamin is a ravenous wolf; in the morning he devours the prey, in the evening he divides the plunder"(Genesis 49:27).

Why Benjamin? Because, Rachel their mother stole a household god *(see home dog)* when she was pregnant with Benjamin. The child Benjamin was thus born with a curse from the *home dog spirit,* which rose to pursue the household god.

The home dog spirit that brood the idol, was overseeing the household of Laban, Rachel's father. The curse lingered in the life of Benjamin for years, but his father Jacob later revealed it prophetically.

Did Benjamin think that, it was a right thing to be possessed by the hunting dog spirit? Is that why he did not bother himself to pray against it? Surely he did not know anything either. See this curse again in the phrase:

"Benjamin is a ravenous wolf; in the morning he devours the prey, in the evening he divides the plunder" (Genesis 49:27).

African Praise Names

In the African community, and according to their traditions, this verse sounds like a praise name for Benjamin surname. Many people do not take time to carefully research about their praise names whether they mean a curse or a blessing. They pass it on to their children.

When a praise name applauded to a person, there are different spirits of dogs that shake themselves up within that person. Some may devour, but some are just mere fearful hunting dogs, ever bullied by the others whenever invoked.

You may wonder why your behaviour is bad and your effects are moving offshore. It is because you love your surname, and praise names too much.

Yet, you do not know where it came from, and how many devils invoked when applauded. Looking at the thousands of years when the spirit of hunting dog was ruling the tribe of Benjamin, until Apostle Paul.

One can realise that any unbroken curse travels for generation to generation. He received his deliverance by the lightning of Lord Jesus on his mission to Damascus where he was going to hunt Christians with the same spirit of a hunting dog, which was on king Saul, the Benjamite.

The Blood of the Martyred Shed by Dogs

It grieved the Holy Spirit to see Stephen; a man of great faith brutally killed whilst under His influence, and preaching the truth to the Jews. Although with the evidence of open heaven, the beast spirited Jews did not see the glory of the LORD. As mentioned earlier, people who are under the influence of the evil spirit of a dog do not shudder at the anointing.

They become stubborn with blocked minds that would not change until it achieves evil. Have you ever seen a person who just wants to quarrel with another just after church, or wants to start a fight at the course of a preacher's sermon? Here is an example as it happened to Stephen:

"Then they cried out with a loud voice, and <u>stopped their ears</u>, and ran upon him with one accord, and cast him out of the city, and stoned him: and **the witnesses laid down their clothes at a young man `s feet, whose name was Saul"** (Acts 7:56-58).

After he was born again, Apostle Paul -then Saul testified about how he was also involved in the killing of Stephen as he was under the influence of the evil spirit of a hunting dog:

"And when the blood of thy martyr Stephen was shed, I also was standing by, and consenting unto his death, and kept the clothing of them that murdered him" (Acts 22:20).

Apostle Paul, being enlightened about his past nature, gave the following warnings to the Philippian church:

"Beware of dogs, beware of evil workers, and beware of the concision." *For we are the circumcision, which worship God in the spirit, and rejoice in Christ Jesus, and have no confidence in the flesh"* (Philippians 3:2-3).

Paul gave this account about his former ways

"For you have heard of my former conduct in Judaism, how I persecuted the church of God beyond measure and tried to destroy it.

And I advanced in Judaism beyond many of my contemporaries in my own nation, being more exceedingly zealous for the traditions of my fathers. But when it pleased God, who separated me from my mother's womb and called me through His grace to reveal His Son in me, that I might preach Him among the Gentiles, I did not immediately confer with flesh and blood, nor did I go up to Jerusalem to those who were apostles before me" (Galatians. 1:13-17).

Pray to break any covenant of a curse with any of the spirits of dogs, which came in through your great, great parents. They are no longer here to confess their sins and repent, but you are suffering from what you do not know. Pray, perhaps the Lord may even reveal it.

Many people have become most of these things which are mentioned early in this chapter, not because they wanted to become that, but because someone senior at home once been that thing –*a captive of this kind of a devil.*

Therefore, that same spirit of a hunting dog lingered to look for someone else to devour. Have a look again at these acts of this spirit and see if you remember a list of people in your family who practised these acts: Ritual murderers, kidnappers, robbers, instigators, backhanders, scammers, fraudsters, human traffickers, slave traders, evil diviners, sorcerers, slanderers, soothsayers, devil worshipers, Satanists, occult leaders, black and white witches, magicians, and wizards.

Are you not also doing the same thing? The Lord Jesus Christ came to set captives free.

Chapter 15

Beware of the Shepherd Dog

(Ancient Wolf, False Prophet)

The Shepherd dog is a religion based devil, which possesses false workers in the church, and false believers wherever there is a spiritual assemble. The evil spirit breeds apostasy amongst brethren, so that they may commit the unpardonable sin of disbelief against the commandments of the LORD.

"The wolf also shall dwell with the lamb" (Isaiah 11:6).

The Shepherd dog wires itself within the spirit of false prophets, sorcerers, mediums. It teaches people how to summon evil spirits to impart them on objects for the purpose of worshiping those objects. The shepherd dog is a wolf that moves about where there is the shepherd in a bid to contend with the Shepherd to deceive and capture the sheep.

This evil spirit of a wolf understands the sheep very well, but the sheep confuses it with the fellow sheep, because it can disguise itself.

It is not easy to recognise a spirit of a shepherd dog in a religious or spiritual person, because religion and spiritual practices are a devout cover, which when put over the shoulders, makes a person to look devout, and yet inside the heart is a ferocious dog.

How do you suspect the man or woman who has a church, calls upon the name of the LORD, or is very close to the prophet or your pastor?

'They come to you in sheep's clothing, but inwardly they are ravenous wolves" (Matthew 7:15).

More details about false prophets are written in my book, which is entitled: *"THE FALSE PROPHET"*

Chapter 16

Beware of Watchdog Spirit (Talebearers)

The watchdog is an evil reporter of crafted, or false bad news. He operates in the spiritual and physical world.

"A talebearer reveals secrets, but he who is of a faithful spirit conceals a matter" (Proverbs 11:13).

The job of this dog spirit is to update the rulers and princes of the underworld about the impact of their evil influence and activities in the world. Unless there is news broadcast, the devil does not know anything. He is not omnipresent like God, but he depends on information from media platforms, and his talebearers.

The watchdog spirit possesses many people who are not necessarily journalists, although it works better with some journalists, because they are easily sold out when motivated by money incentives.

This evil spirit gives them passion to investigate, and snort around for errors, and strictly wrong doings so that they inform about it to the glory of darkness, the doer of evil.

"They return at evening, they howl and snarl like dogs, and go [prowling] about the city. Behold, they belch out [insults] with their mouths; swords [of sarcasm, ridicule, slander, and lies] are in their lips, for who, they think, hears us?

But You, O Lord, will laugh at them [in scorn]; You will hold all the nations in derision. *And at evening let them return; let them howl and snarl like dogs, and go prowling about the city. Let them wander up and down for food and tarry all night if they are not satisfied (not getting their fill)"* (Psalm 59:6-8, 14-15).

Those who are under this kind of devil work hard to defame the character of those who trespass the regulations of the terrestrial domain. This domain regulates the celestial beings, to limit their activities. Truth and righteousness is a crime in the kingdom of darkness.

A watchdog spirit also raises false alarms to distract peace and focus, to cause division and more hatred. A watchdog spirited person is exposed by his false news, and smear campaigns. Watchdogs smear campaigns are for distorting the integrity of a righteous person.

This is because, the prayers and good works of the righteous, are a threat against the evil activities of their masters –the devils. They do this to defame the names of the righteous.

It does not matter to them, how much ravaging damage they cause through their false reports, so long as paid for howling. The watchdog reporters use mass communication platform for spread bad and false news, every day.

"How can you say, "We are wise, and the law of the LORD is with us, when actually the lying pen of the scribes has written lies" (Jeremiah 8:8).

This watchdog spirit will soon spread false news that Christ has come. The news will broadcast here, and there, claiming that, Jesus had been seen. Yet, He has given the saints clear signs of His coming. The Lord Jesus warned about the fake news:

"If anyone says to you, "Look, here is the Christ!" or "there!" Do not believe it" (Matthew 24:23).

Be careful of the news that the media spread against the Gospel of Jesus Christ. Do you think they can always report the truth about what they do not believe? Those possessed by this watchdog energy use interchanged words that prove their story was a lie, such as: Alleged, so-called, claims, rumour, suspected.

These words come from the family of lies: Defamation, slander, libel, character assassination, scandal mongering, malicious gossip, abuse, backbiting, derogation, insult, smear campaign, bad mouthing.

The only time a story is almost accurate is when the wolf has shed blood, stolen or destroyed through murder, accidents, natural disasters, and robbery.

Where have you seen a telecast broadcasting good news except the Christian preaching broadcast? A newspaper running a headline about murder, rape, robbery, strikes and riots, deadly fires, plane crashes, crimes and political clashes sells better than the one, which talks about donation to the poor.

The devil is not by any means interested in promoting anyone doing good works. He wants to hear that someone has done evil, or something bad has happened. This evil spirit called watchdog works with the sea dog spirit to source out money.

Notice that a journalist can easily walk away with a lump sum of money for threatening his prey about a bad report. Understand that for a journalist to get good money, he/she must write about really eye raising stories, and there comes in the lies. Someone must always be there to pay a journalist for the stories they write.

The watchdog spirit in the days of Jesus

False news did not begin with the new age journalists. In biblical times, these were gathering news, and writing down. They were known as, "Scribes." If the Lord Jesus was living on earth in the time of the new age media and company of watch dogs, this same headline would have run on all the media platforms and spread throughout the world to hinder people from believing in Him: The scribes who came down from Jerusalem said;

"He has Beelzebub," and, "By the ruler of demons He casts out demons" (Mark 3:22).

Nevertheless, praise be to God for defence, somebody else took the tarnishing headlines of the watchdogs against Jesus. He rewrote the story with balanced facts from the side of Jesus. He defended himself:

"How can Satan cast out Satan? If Satan has risen up against himself, and is divided, he cannot stand, but has an end" (Mark 3:27).

In whatever persecution you go through on the hands of the media's watchdog spirit; remember that the Lord promised to defend you.

"I will give you a mouth and a wisdom which all your adversaries will not be able to contradict or resist" (Luke 21:15).

When you follow through the Life of Jesus Christ, you find that He won all His battles by practising the scriptures. Moreover, in the case above, He did what is written in the book of Isaiah 54:17:

"Every tongue which rises against you, you shall condemn." Therefore, the Lord answered the Scribes: *"Assuredly, I say to you, all sins will be forgiven the sons of men, and whatever blasphemies they may utter; "but he who blasphemes against the Holy Spirit never has forgiveness, but is subject to eternal condemnation.* Because they said, "He has an unclean spirit" (Mark 3:29).

The curse in the work of a watchdog

There is no blessing in tail bearing at all. Therefore, the scribes did not just walk away free after spreading false reports about the Son of God. Nor wonder why some returned later in secret to ask for deliverance from the Lord.

What stories do you spread? Is there not fair reporting? There is accurate and fair reporting on the media but it is very rare.

You must apply your good codes to your journalistic genres, when you write about the dealings of a "man" as a person. Be factual, and let him have his say, without implicating the Gospel, because it is the purest power of God, and the genuine good news. The news of the world troubles the soul, but the good news of the Gospel revives the soul, spirit, and body.

"Beautiful upon the mountains are **the feet of him who bring good news,** *who* **publish peace,** *who brings good news"*(Isaiah 52:7).

Chapter 17

Beware of Street Dog Spirit

The street dog is an unclean infernal power that rests upon people's will power to give them a rebellious hard heart that shuts away from the Spirit of righteousness to **WORLDLY PLEASURE.**

This evil spirit has different captives placed under separate classes and cords. They are corded (tied with ropes), and marked according to their depth, or levels of spirit of devils.

This evil spirit opens to demons of revelry/ debauchery/ festivity as part of their life cycles. This devil and its demons are more active on particular peak times of the day/ months and seasons of the year like Christmas.

Those are the times they replicate themselves into man in various forms. So that, people may spend time indulging in the flesh, and distanced from the light.

This devil was leading the army of the fallen angels who took wives on earth and brought forth troublesome giants. They introduced beauty and entertainment to the people, until Noah's flood.

"Then the LORD saw that the wickedness of man was great upon the earth, and that every inclination of the thoughts of his heart was altogether evil all the time. And the LORD regretted that He had made man on the earth, and it grieved Him in His heart" (Genesis 6:5-6).

End Time Leader of Anarchy and Deception

The street dog spirit through its force and power of indulgence to entertainment and gluttony, *'Let's eat, drink and be merry'*, will lead thousands upon thousands of people who will be caught unaware by the Lord Jesus at His return.

This is the evil spirit of the devil, which will cause many to fall into the trap as the Lord Jesus warned:

"For as in the days of Noah were, so also will be the coming of the Son of man be. For as in the days before the flood, they were eating and marrying and giving in marriage, until the day that Noah entered the ark, and did not know until the flood came and took them away, so also will the coming of the Son of Man be" (Matthew 24:37-42).

A born again believer in Christ Jesus must be aware of the calendar and dates marked for festivity like Christmas, not to partake in their perverted and pagan practices.

Such holidays were through the enemy's trickery created so that also the believers may get used to worldly pleasure.

Then, almost no one will be spared when the Lord Jesus returns and finding His people partying and eating to gratify themselves.

If Christmas day was the day of the Lord Jesus and celebrated in this perverted fashion, why did the early church Apostles, and Christians never commemorate it?

Nevertheless, to fulfil scriptures as the Lord Jesus said in the above verse of what will happen.

Then, such days like Christmas are created so that, the power of sin may fully function. Then, believers may fall into apostasy until the return of the Lord. When devils of festivity have overpowered the minds and hearts of the people, none of them wants to hear about repentance and eternal destruction.

Like in the days of Noah, this evil spirit causes people to think that there will be no such a thing as the end of their pleasure. That is why Gospel revivals to preach redemption are hindered by the street dog spirit during festive seasons.

Even churches run casual prayer meetings on such days, because, the minds of the people are overpowered by the evil spirit of the street dog, to lead them to entertainment and apostasy.

This hardship faced by true preachers of the gospel of Jesus Christ on such days of festivity is exactly what the Noah the preacher of righteousness faced in those days where people were busy with entertainment *-enjoying the passing world* until the last day where there was no more chance to repent.

"Watch therefore, for you do not know what hour your Lord is coming" "Therefore you also be ready, for the Son of Man is coming at an hour you do not expect" (Matthew 24:42, 44)

This kind of evil dog leads people to deeper deception: Lies, dishonesty, disloyalty, fake friends.

Therefore, many people today have fake friends who have coned them through social media.

Some have fallen to fake love that has led them to ravenous relationships and marriages which rippled them in the end.

There are more of fakes to attract and deceive the real through social media these days: Fake hips, fake buttocks, fake breasts, fake hair, fake nails, fake eyelashes, fake money, fake bank accounts, fake online pages, fake labels, fake identity etc. All this is because of the power of the street dog.

The street dog replicate itself into the following kinds of lifestyles of people: Drunkard, reveller, secular music composer, entertainment celebrity, prostitute, satanic beauticians, undressed model, seductive fashion designer, gays, gangsters, bestial rapist, lesbian, homosexual, pornographic star, adultery, child molester, seductive dancer, same sex marriages, fornicators and sexpartite or masturbation vessels.

People who are also addicted to eating and drinking none health or strange things are possessed by this kind of evil spirit of a dog.

There are also those who are addicted to prescription drugs, marijuana, crystal meth, alcohol, crack, cocaine, or even heroin.

The only purpose of this unclean spirit is to use people to spread their focus on worldly pomp and self-gratification, whilst wasting their time, so that their days may be shorter.

These are best lovers of self and money. After using a person, the devil strips off all his/her glory, and cast him into the bowels of hell. Therefore, there are people living in hell whilst here in the world. This evil spirit removes godly fear from people, and breathes blasphemy, that eventually leads mental disturbances, and poverty.

"Don't copy the behaviour and customs of this world, but let God transform you into a new person

by changing the way you think. Then you will learn to know God's will for you, which is good and pleasing and perfect" (Romans 12:2).

It wears your clothes

The street dog influences people to love themselves maintain a particular status, look, and dress code. Some people would not know why they like to shape their head and paint their faces like that.

What do the eyes of a bat have to do with a woman? It is not sin to dress smart and look good as a person, or to dress according to your level.

For example, a king, queen, and princes are expected to dress according to their status. It can become an insult to society for a king to dress himself like any other man in public.

How much more dignified should be the kings, and priests of the kingdom of God. Are you supposed to dress yourself like a prostitute to prove to the world, that Jesus has given you freedom to do anything? No ways!

The way you look good, shows how happy and at rest your heart is.

A person who is under distress will definitely dress in a confused fashion just to cover his or her body. Forgive him/her. Your face, hair, and shoes may either reveal the distress of your spirit, or its happiness. Nevertheless, beware, that it depends on the source of your upliftment or joy.

If your joy comes from the Lord, you will know how to present your Lord through your outward appearance with a modest dress code that does not appeal to this devil of lust.

You need not to walk around in town in a tight mini skirt or denims and half top in order to express your joy and freedom in the Lord Jesus. This unclean spirit anoints some fashion designers.

It uses their minds to design seductive patterns to promote perversion and lust through sexual immoral clothing fashion.

The devil is thus represented in the dress code, hairstyle, make up and a language. Many simple men have fallen on the trap of the street dog spirit through women who wear flesh enticing clothes.

The dogs have bitten them, and their bones have become piles of logs ready for the Hell fire. This evil spirit of a street dog causes people to become a dry branch that falls away from Christ.

How some are initiated?

Most of those possessed by this unclean spirit are producers of every entertainment programs that appeal to people with worldly indulgence.

These are pornographic films, most secular movies, worldly music videos, some TV shows, dances, social clubs, social drinking spots, the wrestlers and fighters, prostitutes' business and some carton programs.

The street dog spirit works with a host of demons of lust called initiators. These use the skills in these mentioned things to initiate people to practise the same things.

These unclean spirits through films had possessed many people. You say you do not go to the nightclub, or commit adultery. But, you enter the nightclub at the comfort of your house; and fornicate with people right through your flat screen TV, computer.

Some even through their smart phones connect to masturbation. See how tricky is the street dog, and its demons. A simple 5 (five) seconds video can initiate a viewer to do what he has seen. A demonic song can carry your emotions away to sin.

"My son, if sinners entice you, turn your back on them" (Proverbs 1:10).

It is unfortunate that Christian's children who go to study media, do not apply their thoughts, and mind to the Holy Spirit to create concepts that can tell a story about the Kingdom of God, expose the works of Satan, and influence all people to follow Christ.

Instead, they come back from their training to join the enemy in spreading perversity by acting in demonic films and TV programs. They answer the wicked calling to become devil's superstars. It does not matter how much you are paid for acting that character.

Although every Sunday you go to church, but if the character you play on the movie has led thousands of people to fall into sin, temptation, and initiated by this devil, how much destruction have you done to their souls? I have heard many people who said, they felt an urge to masturbate after watching a TV Soapy, which had half-nude scenes. If you are Christian refrain from worldly movies and soapy. They will wash away all the oil of the Holy Spirit from you, and you will get dry.

"Whoever is not with me is against me, and whoever does not gather with me scatters" (Matthew 12:30).

Spiritual husbands and wives

It is through the street dog principalities where demons were born through the generation of the vagabond descendants of Cain (Genesis 6).

"*Now when men began to multiply on the face of the earth and daughters were born to them, the sons of God saw that the daughters of men were beautiful, and they took as wives whomever they chose"*(Genesis 6:1-2).

Even today, people possessed by the street dog spirit have spiritual husbands, and spiritual wives as others still give birth to demons and strange beings in the spirit world and in real life. That is why these can assign spells of demons to go for an assignment because demons are their children. You might have noticed how it is much easy to cast out a demon, than it is to deal with wicked human beings – there is a beast behind (a dog).

Street dogs spirit routines

Most people who are possessed by a street dog spirit like moving out of their homes to hang out with fellows from 3 PM in the afternoon, and they are comfortable to return in the early hours of the morning, if they ever decide to return.

In the night, they roam around the cities where there is entertainment, or lie in wait for one that they can devour. Social media has made it easier for most of them to network and connect, and roam around the world at the comfort of their homes.

"Strive to save others, snatching [them] out of [the] fire; on others take pity [but] with fear, loathing even the garment spotted by the flesh and polluted by their sensuality" (Jude 1:23) [Zech. 3:2-4].

It is not every prayer that goes here, unless he/she wants to be born again. Be careful not to drain out your spiritual life holding hands and praying with a person who spends time in street dog activities. Apostle Paul warned the Corinthian church about Christians who are of such nature.

"I write to you not to associate with anyone who bears the name of [Christian] brother if he is known to be guilty of immorality or greed, or is an idolater [whose soul is devoted to any object that usurps the place of God], or is a person with a foul tongue [railing, abusing, reviling, slandering], or is a drunkard or a swindler or a robber. You must not

so much as eat with such a person" (1 Corinthians 5:11).

These double minded fellows, after wasting your time praying with them, they return to their houses to glue their eyes on those accursed materials.

If you return to the things you say you flush out after watching, how much toxic is your spirit? They want breakthroughs, but the beast, which they do not want to let go, leads them. There must be a distinction between a Christian, and a pagan. Be one thing.

"Of them the proverbs are true: **"A dog returns to its vomit," and, "A sow that is washed returns to her wallowing in the mud"** (2 Peter 2:22).

Chapter 18

Beware of House / Home Dog

The house /home dog spirit possess people of the same bloodline, and through pagan friendships which bonds for a long time.

"Do not trust in a friend; do not put your confidence in a companion" (Micah 6:5).

This evil spirit lives within the bloodline of family members (DNA). The evil spirit causes some individuals in the family to oversee and to pass on their evil practices, rituals, and demons of destruction within their lineage. Idols of families are influenced by this evil spirit –whether ancestral powers or any other demonic power that is worshiped by the family.

You might remember the story of the man Micah. He had a shrine, and made an ephod and household idols; and he consecrated one of his sons, who became his priest in the shrine (Judges 17:5). Most of the time, the home dog spirit demands for an animal, or human blood sacrifice.

It says it is hungry and wants to be appeased so that it may bless the family. Nevertheless, after the sacrifice or food, it broils more hardship to the participants.

It is all deception of Satan to cause families and tribes to become his frantic captives. Jesus Christ offered His lifeblood once and for all. There is no need for more blood to make you free! Kick away that dog spirit from your house!

Most family names *(surnames)* and praise names have a chain linking the family members to the home dog spirit. The home dogs work day and night to monitor family member's movements.

They also place evil eyes on each one of them whenever they choose to follow Jesus Christ.

This is the spirit, which tells people that; *"In our home we don't worship this, we worship this, so you must not go there."*

They want to confine you to a particular routine, which is common among those in their limited circles. It pursued the Lord Jesus to sit Him down and limit Him, but He shook it off.

"But when His own people heard about this, they went out to lay hold of Him, for they said, He is out of His mind"(Mark 3:21).

Contempt and reproach usually comes from this kind of an evil spirit. This is the kind of evil spirit, which will never want to see you lifted up and prospering in your life. It works out means to waste you away and keep you stagnant just for control.

If there begins change or improvement in your life, it barks at you –through your family members.

Therefore, some people once they travel to visit their hometowns or villages they come back bitten by the home dog and things begin to fall apart.

"A man's enemies are the men of his own household"(Micah 6:6).

Prayerful Christians are worst hated by the home/housedog. In large homesteads, there is always one person who is used by the home dog, or suspected to be one. There are those falsely accused of witchcraft, or casting spells of curses on some family members.

Yet, the housedog spirit is just using him or her as a scapegoat. However, there are those who know that they are under the power of this devil and they bewitch family members and relatives or members of the community.

You must hide under the wings of the shadow of the Most High to be protected from a housedog. The home dog hates prayer and prophecy to the extent that it can rage and bark throughout. It pursues the people who pray until they leave prayer or backslide. Some people ever since they became Christians, life became a warzone, and hardship pursued them at home.

There is a home dog evil spirit ravaging behind the scenes. Break away from the chains of the home dog and enjoy the full package of your redemption through Jesus Christ. Mind your own personal freedom first before you try to pull the other family members.

Make sure that your faith is strong enough to confront the idols in your family. If you yourself are still under the control of a spirit ruling your home and family or community, you cannot deliver others; but instead the dog spirit will ravage your life.

"Then Jesus told them, "A prophet is without honor only in his home town, among his relatives, and in

his own household. So He could not perform any miracles there, except to lay His hands on a few of the sick and heal them" (Mark 6:4-5).

Why do wolves hate prophets? It is because; a shepherd smells different and radiate light through the eyes. That frustrates the dog.

The House/Home dog is a ruling power of darkness specially assigned over homes and houses. It causes righteous people to be connected to wrong people who must become a snare, and a hindrance to their ways of holiness.

For example, the daughter of King Saul who was given by Saul to David (2 Samuel 6:16). God knows all these things, which are practised through this evil spirit in most families.

Therefore, He is always concerned about who relates with His children, and for what purpose. Due to the same cause, LORD warned the children of Israel:

"You shall not make marriages with them; your daughter you shall not give to his son nor shall you take his daughter for your son, *"For they will turn away your sons from following Me, that they may serve other gods; so will the anger of the Lord be kindled against you and He will destroy you quickly"* (Deuteronomy 7:3-4).

Evil spirits can be imparted from one's family to another, and within the family. Unless you cut the ties of the spirit of a home dog, you will not fulfil the original plan of God for your life. Move away!

"For this reason a man will leave his father and mother and be united to his wife, and the two will become one flesh?" (Matthew 19:5).

This devil hinders progress and prosperity, and cause family members to move in circles of similar problems without solutions from generation to the next *(rising and falling).*

As a result, the world has many communities whose members suffer the same problems. Anyone who tries to improve is pulled down by the pack of wolves of this kind. The home dog may become a strongman in a community that rules through leaders.

It attracts a host of demons to levy burdens upon people, and they make it a uniform in the family or community e.g. poverty, inherited diseases, loss of marriages, ant marriage, polygamous marriages, ancestral practises – community of Sangomas (Mediums), drunkenness, deaths of youths, deaths of children, barrenness and the like.

"If anyone is in Christ, he is a new creation; old things have passed away; behold, all things have become new"(2 Corinthians 5:17).

More on the Homedog spirit is found in my book titled: *"The LORD is My Banner"*

Chapter 19

Beware of Intelligent Dog

The intelligent dog is the kind of devil, which rules over all evil crafts that is meant to depressingly affect people. Materially or psychologically devised, the evil crafts are wisely devised, to achieve the following: Deform, kill, terminate, steal, stray, derail, automate, vandalise, and evil modify.

An example may be the latest evil technology used to cause a targeted airplane to lose the aviation signal of the air tower controller, so that it may fly astray to an unknown destination where passengers may be kept hostage, abused and killed to hide evidence.

Possessed by the Intelligent Dog

The intelligent dog possesses minds of people of all age groups, to function through their brains, so that; they may invent any evil technology. More details about the intelligent dog are discussed in my book titled: *The Acts of the Intelligent Dog*.

Chapter 20

Beware of Seadog

The Seadog is the principality, and evil power that controls trade, monies, taxes, illicit riches, and the forbidden accumulation of mammon of the people of the world.

This kind of devil possesses people who are hungry for power, riches, and fame. It leads many to become very poor in heavenly treasures, but to become robbers in order to make riches in the world. God alone has the power to cut off the power of the seadog. It was the same seadog, which confiscated all the riches of Job, and shut down his businesses.

"When your wares came forth from the seas, you met the desire, the demand, and the necessities of many people; you enriched the kings of the earth with your abundant wealth and merchandise. Now you are shattered by the seas in the depths of the waters; your merchandise and all your crew have gone down with you" (Ezekiel 27:2-4, 32-36).

The seadog influenced merchandise in the temple in Jerusalem, Jesus arrived there and rebuked the merchants and said, *"My house shall be called a house of prayer; but you have made it a den of robbers"* (Matthew 21:13).

The traders were selling animal sacrifice, and grain offering in the temple. They were converting the animals to cash, and trading them for higher price to gain profit. That is why the Lord Jesus scattered the money of the moneychangers. These traders were even selling things that are not supposed to be sold, but given free by God.

"Jesus went into the temple and drove out all who bought and sold in the sacred place, and He turned over the four-footed tables of the money changers and the chairs of those who sold doves" (Matthew 21:12).

Today the sea dog spirit has caused the love of money such that, traders sell a cup of water to thirsty travellers. The very same water, which comes from heaven to bless everyone, goes at a very high price for profit.

A person who is possessed by a seadog spirit would not mind how and where his riches or money comes from, as long as it is money. His soul does not rely on the LORD for prosperity, because the power of the seadog gives him dubious ideas of making money.

Therefore, the world has thousands of people who accumulated wealth through illegal and harmful things.   There are people who have become very loaded with money through selling drugs, stealing cars, bribery, slave trading, and by many evil ways. In these days, the influence of the seadog has become higher than in the days of Tyre and Babylon.

"The last days will come perilous times of great stress and trouble [hard to deal with and hard to bear]. *For people will be lovers of self and self-centred, lovers of money and aroused by an inordinate [greedy] desire for wealth, proud and arrogant and contemptuous boasters"* (2 Timothy 3:1-3).

Character of Possessed Persons

A person possessed by this spirit, becomes a hypocrite who changes to one thing there, and wear another facemask somewhere else.

He interchanges characters to charm, and suit every event, because they are under the power of a sea dog spirit influencing them to gain what they want at each time.

A seadog is a very stubborn anti-prayer spirit, with a reinforcing power to block deliverance, so that, the possessed may remain bound. Those possessed by this kind of devil do not confess the Lord Jesus publicly. However, they demand special attention, and acknowledgment for their importance, and presence in the Holy assembles.

Most seadogs spirited people do not worship God in truth, unless somebody must worship on their behalf through the money, which they give. They see worshiping or attending church as a way of doing God a favour or honouring the invite of the host.

They will come to church to show off their presence and big names. They give big money offering and fly away. Although some may attend church services regularly, but most seadogs travel to consult mediums at night somewhere else.

They like doing charitable work of giving to the needy, to gain praise from men, but not to honour God. Their giving is with an attitude to control the needy, or to earn something in return.

"Is it not the rich who domineer over you? Is it not they who drag you into the law courts?" (James 2:6).

The Seadog Power in Businesses

As the Lord Jesus was travelling by sea, He encountered the sea dog; it came against Him through the raging winds that shook the boat. The men were bewildered, and they marvelled, saying,

*"What kind of Man is this, that even the winds and the sea obey Him!" "And when He arrived at the other side in the country of the Gadarenes, **two men under the control of demons** went to meet*

Him, coming out of the tombs, so fierce and savage that no one was able to pass that way" (Matthew 8:28).

This was the spirit of the men, which He met on the other side with the raging wind on the sea. Although the seadog hid its identity by saying, it is "legion," but it begged Jesus,

"Have You come to torment us before the appointed time?"(Matthew 8:29).

Remember that, the devils knew that, the Seed of the woman would come to crush the head of the serpent. Therefore, the seadog knew that the appointed time was coming for Jesus to end their power, which is why it spoke like that through the possessed man.

In this scenario, the seadog devil begged Jesus to send them to the pigs. They rode themselves to the sea where the power of the seadog, which helped the people of Gaderene to do the business of rearing pigs, came from.

That was after all the pigs died there, that the merchants of Gedarenes, asked that Jesus be chased away. Many times a man of God who will expose the evil practices of traders is unwanted in a place.

However, Jesus delivered the man used as a host of the seadog, but the pig business of the people of Gaderen collapsed.

The herdsmen fled and went into the town and reported everything, including what had happened to the men under the power of demons. "And behold, the whole town went out to meet Jesus; and as soon as they saw Him, they begged Him to depart from their locality" (Matthew 8:33-34).

The seadog spirit causes a person to continue to hoard possessions for himself but is not rich in relation to God. As a result, when their time to die comes, it takes them unaware, and they die without being born again, having not even enjoyed their riches.

"For what is the hope of the godless and polluted, even though he has gained [in this world], when God cuts him off and takes away his life? Will God hear his cry when trouble comes upon him?" (Job 27:8-9).

The devil will never let you enjoy what you obtained by his means. He let you heap it up, so that your enemies may enjoy it once you die.

Alternatively, he will make it to blow away from your hand, so that you keep working hard, and forget about building your relationship with the Lord.

God said to him, *"You fool! This very night they [the messengers of God] will demand your soul of you;*

and all the things that you have prepared, whose will they be?" (Luke 12:20).

The seadog spirit is itself the devil of money, and it attracts all marine spirits. To prove to the worldly people that Jesus knew the author of the concept behind money, Jesus sends Peter to go, and collect it from the sea through a fish.

Earthly riches and worldly pursuits do not drive those born of the Spirit of God, because the spirit within them gives them contentment.

They worship God with thanks giving and peace whether in need, or abundant supply. You must understand that, God desires for you to seek His kingdom, and His righteousness first, and then all that you need shall follow you.

"But if we have food and clothing, with these we shall be content (satisfied). As for the rich in this world, charge them not to be proud and arrogant and contemptuous of others, nor to set their hopes

on uncertain riches, but on God, Who richly and ceaselessly provides us with everything for [our] enjoyment"(1 Timothy 6:8, 17).

"Like the partridge that gathers a brood which she did not hatch and sits on eggs which she has not laid, so is he who gets riches by unjust means and not by right. He will leave them, or they will leave him, in the midst of his days, and at his end he will be a fool"(Jeremiah 17:10-11).

The Sea Dog's Power over Tax Collection

The sea dog as god of money is also an evil principality that is responsible for the manipulation of national treasuries.

When you dig through the scriptures, you find that paying tax was a means of slavery levied by kings who had power over colonised nations.

Their subjects, "enslaved nations, or group of foreign people," duly paid these duties to the king's treasury. However, the king's people or his children were tax exempted. We discuss this further in a special edition.

Att: Reader

Have you been helped by this book?

I would love to hear from you. Please send me your comments or questions: lydiaeelyon@gmail.com

Remain Revived

Lydia E'Elyon

Copyright © 2021 by Lydia E'Elyon